SKI TOURS
in the
SIERRA NEVADA

Volume 2
Carson Pass
Bear Valley
Pinecrest

By Marcus Libkind

Bittersweet Publishing Company
Livermore, California

Cover design by Mac Smith.

Front cover photograph by Kim Grandfield.

Rear cover photograph by Lee Griffith.

All other photographs by author unless noted otherwise.

Acknowledgement: Over the years many people have been the source of invaluable information. They include National Forest Service, National Park Service and State Park personnel, the owners and operators of nordic centers and mountain shops, friends, and acquaintances. I am especially indebted to Brian Klimkowsky for his review of the manuscript and his thoughtful comments and ideas. Above all, I must thank Clara Yen for the many hours she spent editing the manuscript.

Library of Congress Catalog Card Number: 84-73452
International Standard Book Number: 0-931255-01-5

Published by Bittersweet Publishing Company
P.O. Box 1211, Livermore, California 94550

Printed in the United States of America

To

my friends

with whom I have shared many adventures

Contents

BEAR VALLEY

PINECREST

Introduction

The guidebook series, *Ski Tours in the Sierra Nevada*, forms a comprehensive collection of ski tours which I have encountered during more than a decade of exploring the Sierra. They range geographically from the Lake Tahoe region in the north to Sequoia National Park in the south. The Lake Tahoe, Carson Pass, Bear Valley, Pinecrest, Yosemite, Huntington and Shaver Lakes, Kings Canyon and Sequoia areas are all covered in depth.

Whether you are a novice or an old timer, this series of guidebooks will introduce you to new and interesting areas which offer excellent ski touring opportunities. The information in these volumes will be useful for planning tours of an appropriate difficulty so you can enjoy more pleasurable and safer touring.

The 59 tours in this volume cover a large geographical area and are divided as follows:

> CARSON PASS—Tours originating from or near Highway 88. Also those from Highway 89 east of Luther Pass.

> BEAR VALLEY—Tours originating from or near Highway 4 west of Ebbetts Pass.

> PINECREST—Tours originating from or near Highway 108 west of Sonora Pass.

I sincerely hope that the tours in these guidebooks will inspire you to explore new areas. I have thoroughly enjoyed the time spent in researching these books and I will be rewarded each time I meet another ski tourer who has found this information useful. As I would like to hear from you, let me know your comments and suggestions.

Marcus Libkind
P.O. Box 1211
Livermore, California 94550

Author's Note

There are certain inherent dangers associated with wilderness travel in winter. No guidebook can diminish the hazards nor be a guarantee of safety. If you choose to experience the mountains in winter, you voluntarily do so knowing there are hazards.

Although the tour descriptions make reference to specific, obvious dangers, you should not assume that they are the only ones. Even the safest tour can become dangerous should you encounter poor weather, or adverse snow or avalanche conditions.

Some tours may take you through private property which is not marked. If you encounter marked private property, I hope that you will respect the property rights of others so that the good reputation of ski tourers will be preserved. Similarly, some tours pass through downhill ski resorts. For safety and to promote continued goodwill it is important to stay off the groomed slopes when ascending.

Although great care has gone into researching the tours in this guidebook, you may find inconsistencies due to factors such as new construction of roads and housing, policies toward plowing roads, changes in parking restrictions, and changes in trail markers. Also, extreme variations in snowfall can make a remarkable difference in how things appear. Be prepared to cope with these discrepancies should they arise.

In the final analysis, you must be responsible for executing your own safe trip.

Great snow, great weather and great companions

How To Use This Book

The short time it takes you to read this section will increase the usefulness of this guidebook. Each tour description in this guidebook contains a summary and a narrative. The summary box gives you at a glance the significant characteristics of the tour. The narrative is a description of the route.

Below is an explanation of each characteristic in the summary box.

Difficulty: The difficulty ratings are based on four criteria: length, elevation change, steepness, and navigation. A 5 level scale for rating the overall difficulty of the tours is used. The skills associated with each level are:

1—Beginner

- Little or no previous ski touring experience
- Follow simple directions without map or compass

2—Advancing beginner

- Proficiency in the basic techniques: diagonal stride, sidestep, kick turn, step turn, snowplow and snowplow turn
- Control speed on gradual downhills
- Negotiate short moderately steep terrain
- Follow simple directions in conjunction with a map

3—Intermediate

- Excellent proficiency in all the basic techniques plus the traverse and herringbone on moderately steep terrain
- Negotiate long moderately steep and short steep terrain
- Good stamina
- Navigate using a topographic map
- Use a compass to determine general orientation

4—Advancing intermediate

- Excellent proficiency in all ski touring techniques
- Negotiate long steep terrain including densely wooded areas
- Strong skier
- Navigate using a topographic map and compass

5—Expert

- Excellent all around ski tourer and mountain person
- Negotiate very steep terrain
- Exceptional endurance
- Navigate using a topographic map and compass

Two tours may be assigned the same rating but vary greatly in the skills required. For example, a tour on a road which is long and a tour which is short but requires navigation by map and compass may both be rated 3. For this reason the difficulty ratings should only be used as a general guide for selecting a tour of appropriate difficulty. Check the summary box for information regarding length, elevation and navigation to determine whether your abilities match the demands of a tour. Also, refer to the narrative which describes the tour route for special considerations.

The tours were rated assuming ideal snow conditions. Deep powder will make the traveling slower and more difficult. Ice, sometimes referred to as "Sierra cement," will make all tours much more difficult. If you are faced with icy conditions you might consider waiting until early afternoon to begin when hopefully the snow will have thawed.

Length: The length is an estimate of the horizontal mileage as obtained from the topographic maps. Several of the tours are in meadows which are adjacent to plowed roads and in these cases the length is simply stated as "short." Also noted is whether the distance is one-way or round trip.

Elevation: The first number is the elevation at the starting point of the tour in feet above sea level. The elevation is a major consideration when planning tours early or late in the season.

The elevation at the starting point is followed by a slash and the elevation change for the entire tour. The change is written as " + gain, − loss." "Nil" is used where the change is negligible.

Navigation: The navigational difficulty of each tour is based on untracked snow and good visibility. The key words and phrases are:

Adjacent to plowed road—Tour is located almost completely within sight of a plowed road.

Road—Tour follows snow-covered roads. Although roads are normally easy to follow, a small road or a road in open terrain may be difficult to locate or follow.

Marked trail—Tour follows marked trail; may require basic map-reading skills. Markers are normally brightly colored pieces of metal attached well above the snow level to trees or strips of brightly colored ribbon attached to tree branches close to the trail. Blazes which mark summer trails are not considered markers since they are often obscured by snow. In nearly all cases, when on a marked trail you must pay careful attention to locating each successive marker which may not be ideally placed. Even with a marked trail, you will probably need some knowledge of the route and basic map-reading skills to follow it.

Map—Tour requires the ability to read a topographic map since the tour follows well-defined terrain such as creeks, valleys, and ridges. Also remember that poor visibility can make route-finding impossible without a compass and expert knowledge of its use.

Compass—Tour requires the use of a compass in conjunction with a topographic map. In some instances the compass is mainly for safety but other routes require you to follow compass bearings.

Round Top from Markleeville Peak   *Bill Rose*

Time: To give you a general idea of the length of time required to complete a tour, I have used the following key words and phrases:

- Short
- Few hours
- Half day
- Most of a day
- Full day
- Very long day
- One very long day or two days

Some of the factors which will affect your trip time include snow and weather conditions, your skiing ability and physical strength, characteristics of the tour, and your personal habits. Consideration has been given to reasonable rests and route finding in making the estimates.

Always keep in mind that the mid-winter months are filled with short days. Very long tours are best done in early spring when the days are longer.

Season: The season is the period in an average snowfall year during which the snow conditions for the tour are acceptable. Early and late in the season the conditions may be less than optimum. Exceptionally early or late snowfall as well as heavy snowfall, extend the season. On the other hand, during drought years the season may be shortened.

Spring skiing at its best

USGS topo: Listed are the United States Geological Survey topographic maps, both scale and name, which cover the tour route. Parts of these maps are reproduced in this guidebook, and the map reproduction number and its page location are at the beginning of each tour adjacent to the tour name. Be aware that some of these maps have been reduced.

For a majority of the tours only the 15′ series maps are listed. The 7.5′ series are also listed if they have significant benefit. When the elevations given for peaks are different on the two map series, the elevations stated in the text are from the map series reproduced in this book.

Topographic Map Legend

●	Starting point
▲	Destination
5	Landmark number (corresponds to narrative)
▬▬	Highway or plowed road
▬ ▬	Ski route

If you desire to purchase maps by mail you can obtain price and ordering information by contacting:

United States Geological Survey
Box 25286 Denver Federal Building
Denver, Colorado 80225

Start and end: Described are detailed directions for locating the starting and ending points of the tour. The ending point is omitted if the tour route returns to where it began.

Keep in mind that it may not be legal to park at these points. Increased usage and recent heavy snowfalls have resulted in greater restrictions and stricter enforcement. Sometimes carrying a snow shovel will allow you to clear a place to park. At other times you may have to resort to paying for parking or walking some distance. In the near future, the California "Sno-Park" bill should provide some relief from this situation.

The remainder of each tour description is in narrative form and describes the route. Keep in mind that the description is not a substitute for knowledge, skill and common sense. For your convenience, when a reference is made to the directions given in a different tour, the name of the tour is followed by the number, e.g. "Meiss Lake tour (no. 20)." Also, significant landmarks mentioned in the text are followed by a number in parentheses which corresponds to the same number found on the map, e.g. "From here descend to a road junction (**4**)."

Backcountry solitude   *Bob Bastasz*

14

Carson Pass

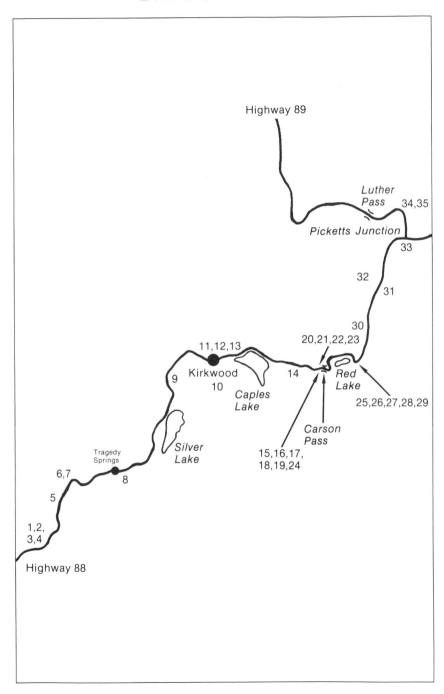

Highway 89

Luther Pass

Picketts Junction

34,35

33

32

31

30

20,21,22,23

11,12,13

Kirkwood

14

Red Lake

9

10

Caples Lake

25,26,27,28,29

Tragedy Springs

Silver Lake

Carson Pass

6,7

8

15,16,17, 18,19,24

5

1,2, 3,4

Highway 88

1 **Foster Meadow**

MAP 1
PAGE 17

Difficulty	1
Length	3 miles round trip
Elevation	7050/ + 250, − 250
Navigation	Road
Time	Few hours
Season	December through mid-April
USGS topo	15′ series, Silver Lake, Leek Spring Hill; 7.5′ series, Bear River Reservoir, Peddler Hill
Start	Highway 88, 3.2 miles northeast of the Bear River Reservoir turnoff and 4.2 miles southwest of Iron Mountain Road. A turnout is located on the north side of the road.

This tour to Foster Meadow is perfect for beginners because it follows a road and the terrain is easy. If you have enjoyed touring to Woods Lake but are tired of the crowds, you will like skiing in this area which is less used.

From the starting point, ski on the road which heads north. At 0.1 mile you will pass a road on your right (**1**). Continue descending down the main road until you have reached the Middle Fork of the Cosumnes River (**2**). You are now 1.0 mile from the start.

At the Middle Fork two roads intersect the main road. On this side of the river, the southeast side, a road heads southwest (left). Take this road and ski 0.5 mile to the edge of Foster Meadow. The meadow is a perfect place to have lunch. If you have more energy you can also explore its 0.5 mile length as well as the surrounding area.

16

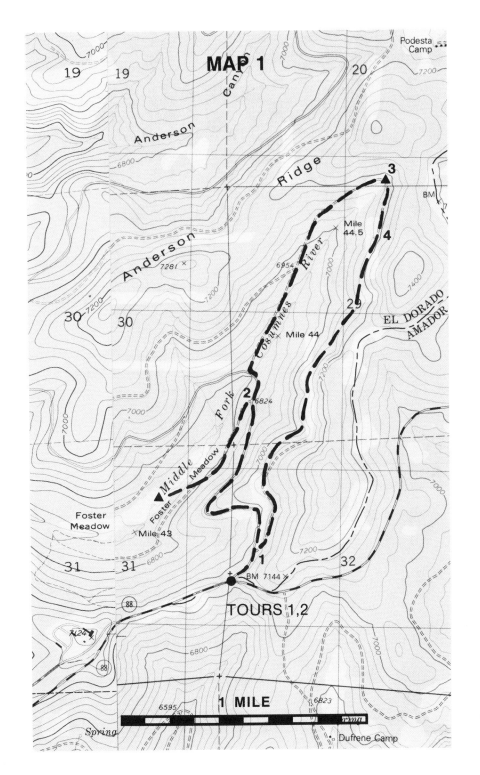

MAP 1

19   19   20

Podesta Camp

Anderson

Ridge

3

BM

Mile 44.5

4

6954

Anderson

7281

6824

Mile 44

EL DORADO
AMADOR

29

30   30

7000

2

Middle

Fork

Foster Meadow

Foster Meadow

Mile 43

1

BM 7144

31   31

32

88

TOURS 1,2

7124

88

1 MILE

6595

6823

Spring

Dufrene Camp

Many roads crisscross the Leek Spring Hill area

MAP 1
PAGE 17

Middle Fork of the Cosumnes River

2

Difficulty	2−3
Length	4 miles round trip
Elevation	7050/ + 600, − 600
Navigation	Road (Road and map for more difficult route)
Time	Half day
Season	December through mid-April
USGS topo	15′ series, Silver Lake; 7.5′ series, Bear River Reservoir
Start	Highway 88, 3.2 miles northeast of the Bear River Reservoir turnoff and 4.2 miles southwest of Iron Mountain Road. A turnout is located on the north side of the road.

This tour leads to the headwaters of the Middle Fork of the Cosumnes River. Like the tour to Foster Meadow, this route is well-suited to beginners in search of a little solitude. More advanced skiers may choose the alternate loop route or the Cosumnes-Anderson Loop tour.

From the starting point, ski on the road which heads north. At 0.1 mile you will pass a road on your right (**1**). Continue descending down the main road until you reach the Middle Fork of the Cosumnes River (**2**). You are now 1.0 mile from the start.

Just before the river is a road which heads southwest (left) to Foster Meadow. Do not take this road. Instead, cross the river and take the road which heads northeast (right) and parallels the Middle Fork. In the next 1.0 mile you will climb 350′ to the headwaters (**3**). Here, you will find an open area that is perfect for lunch and a rest before you begin the return trip.

If you are concerned about difficulty, you can retrace your route back to the starting point. Intermediate skiers who seek some adventure can return via a different route, thus making this tour a loop.

To make the loop. From the open area at the headwaters cross the river and continue south on the road. You will reach the end of the road in 0.2 mile (**4**).

Continue skiing in the same direction (south). This route will lead you through the trees as you traverse along the west side of a ridge. While traversing you should lose elevation very gradually. The rate at which you lose elevation will determine the location where you intersect the main road which you skied from the starting point. Whichever route you choose, you may encounter what appear to be several abandoned logging roads. Only follow them if they head south or southwest.

Once you reach the main road simply follow it back to the starting point.

19

3 Anderson Ridge

MAP 2
PAGE 21

Difficulty	3
Length	9 miles round trip
Elevation	7050/ + 1300, − 1300
Navigation	Road and map
Time	Full day
Season	December through mid-April
USGS topo	15′ series, Silver Lake, Leek Spring Hill; 7.5′ series, Bear River Reservoir, Peddler Hill
Start	Highway 88, 3.2 miles northeast of the Bear River Reservoir turnoff and 4.2 miles southwest of Iron Mountain Road. A turnout is located on the north side of the road.

This tour includes a traverse along the top of Anderson Ridge and allows you to get away from the countless roads which crisscross the area. The terrain along the ridge is rolling and it is a pleasant place to ski slowly and enjoy the solitude of the woods.

From the highway, ski north on the snow-covered road. At 0.1 mile you will pass a road on your right (1). Continue descending down the main road until you reach the Middle Fork of the Cosumnes River (2). You are now 1.0 mile from the start. Here, you will find intersecting roads leading to either Foster Meadow or the headwaters of the Middle Fork.

Cross the Middle Fork of the Cosumnes River and continue for 1.7 miles on the road that you have been following until you reach a prominent point (3). This spot will offer you a fine view of the foothills below.

At this point you will also find a junction with a road heading east (right). Take this road and follow it for 2.0 miles. In this section you will parallel Anderson Ridge to its north, and will climb and drop several times. At one point you will come within 75 vertical feet of the ridge top. At the end of this section you will reach a saddle (4).

At the saddle, leave the road behind and climb to the south until you reach a high point (5). From here, head southwest and traverse along the top of Anderson Ridge for 1.8 miles until you intersect the road on which you started this tour (6).

Once on the road ski southeast (left) until you reach the starting point.

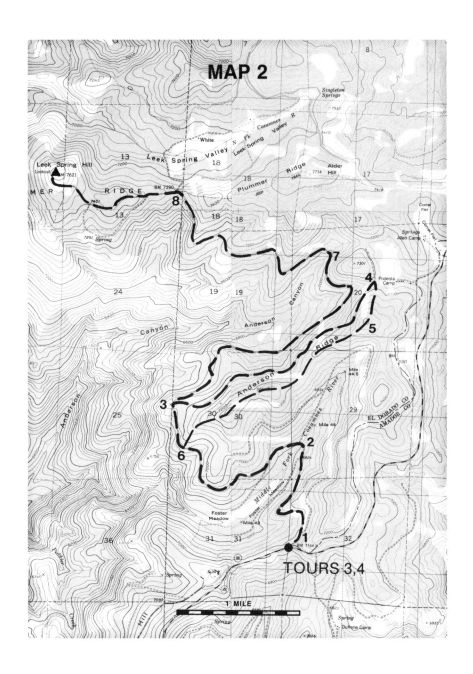

MAP 2

TOURS 3,4

1 MILE

21

4 Leek Spring Hill from Highway 88

MAP 2
PAGE 21

Difficulty	3
Length	16 miles round trip
Elevation	7050/ + 1350, − 1350
Navigation	Road
Time	Full day
Season	December through mid-April
USGS topo	15′ series, Silver Lake, Leek Spring Hill; 7.5′ series, Bear River Reservoir, Peddler Hill, Leek Spring Hill
Start	Highway 88, 3.2 miles northeast of the Bear River Reservoir turnoff and 4.2 miles southwest of Iron Mountain Road. A turnout is located on the north side of the road.

The panoramic view from the lookout atop Leek Spring Hill is enough to entice anyone on this tour. The lookout is situated just above the foothills and the view in all directions is superb. The landmarks include Pyramid Peak and the Crystal Range to the north, Thimble Peak and Round Top to the east, and Mokelumne Peak to the south.

The route described here is not the shortest route to the lookout but it is a beautiful one which is easy to follow and has little gradient and low usage. A shorter route is described in the Leek Spring Hill from Iron Mountain Road tour. If a shuttle car is available you can combine the tour from Highway 88 with the tour from Iron Mountain Road to create an excellent one-way tour which is 12 miles long.

The route to Leek Spring Hill from Highway 88 is very straightforward. Ski on the road which leaves the north side of the highway and winds around for 7.0 miles to where it intersects the Leek Spring Hill from Iron Mountain Road tour at a point denoted by BM 7290 on the topo (**8**). This distance is filled with long stretches of very gradual ups and downs.

As you ski on the road from the highway you will encounter several side roads and drainages which you can use as landmarks. At a point 0.1 mile from the start you will pass a road on your right (**1**) and at 1.0 mile two roads intersect the main road at the Middle Fork of the Cosumnes River (**2**). One heads southwest to Foster Meadow and the other northeast to the headwaters of the Middle Fork.

At 2.7 miles from the start the route passes a prominent point (**3**). Here the slopes drop steeply to the west and a view of the foothills lies before you. At the same point you also pass a road on your right.

At 5.2 miles from the start you will reach a drainage (**7**) where a road and trail heading northeast will be marked. You should continue on the main road which crosses two more drainages until you intersect another road **(8)** which is part of the Leek Spring Hill from Iron Mountain Road tour.

From this junction follow the road to the west (left) for 1.2 miles to the lookout atop Leek Spring Hill. Along this section you will pass two roads on your left.

Breaking trail

5 Cosumnes-Anderson Loop

MAP 3
PAGE 25

Difficulty	3
Length	7 miles round trip
Elevation	7100/ + 750, − 750
Navigation	Road and map
Time	Full day
Season	December through mid-April
USGS topo	15′ series, Silver Lake, Leek Spring Hill; 7.5′ series, Bear River Reservoir, Peddler Hill
Start	Highway 88 near Allen Camp, 6.5 miles northeast of the Bear River Reservoir turnoff and 1.0 mile southwest of Iron Mountain Road. A turnout is located on the west side of the road.

This loop covers parts of the Middle Fork of the Cosumnes River and Anderson Ridge tours. Most of the tour described here is on roads although you can avoid part of the roads by traversing the top of Anderson Ridge. This variation is just a hint of the many loops and one-way tours which can be made in this area.

Ski on the road which heads west from the starting point. A very short distance from the highway, maybe 50 yards, you will find a snow-covered road heading south (left). Follow this road for 0.3 mile until you reach a junction (1). The road to the west (right) leads to the cabins at Podesta Camp. Take note of it as you will return to the junction via this road at the conclusion of the tour.

Continue south (straight) on the road which parallels the highway for 0.6 mile until you reach a fairly large clearing (2) and the road disappears. At this point the route turns west (right). Pick your own route up to the saddle (3) located between two high points.

From the saddle it is not difficult to find a good route down to the west. Follow the slopes which funnel down to the headwaters of the Middle Fork of the Cosumnes River. When the terrain begins to level you will encounter a clearing; locate a road at its northeast end (4).

Ski on the road while paralleling the river on its northwest (right) side. You will lose 350′ in the next 1.0 mile. In this section you will pass a road on your right at 0.5 mile and at 1.0 mile you will intersect another road (5).

At this second road junction a left turn will lead to Highway 88. Instead, turn right and follow the road for 1.7 miles to a prominent point (6) which overlooks the foothills. Here, you will also find a road heading east (right) from the road you are on. Follow this road as it leads to the northeast and parallels Anderson Ridge.

After skiing 2.0 miles you will reach a saddle (**7**) at the north end of Anderson Ridge. These last 2.0 miles on the road can be replaced by a route along the top of Anderson Ridge.

Once at the saddle it is a simple matter to ski east a short distance through the trees to a large meadow. Ski to the southeast corner of the meadow and locate the road near the cabins. This is Podesta Camp. Ski east on this road until you reach an intersection with another road (**1**). Turn north (left) here and ski 0.3 mile to the starting point.

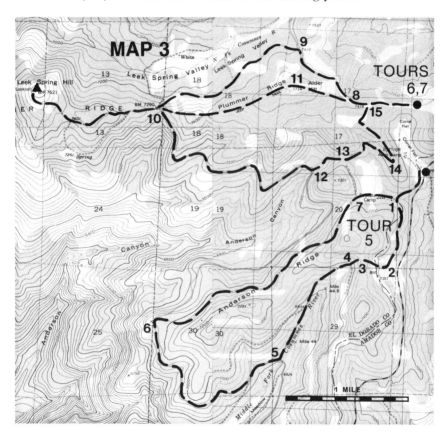

Difficulty	2–3
Length	8 miles round trip
Elevation	7250/+650, −650 (7250/+1150, −1150 by Plummer Ridge)
Navigation	Road (Road and map for Plummer Ridge route)
Time	Most of a day
Season	December through mid-April
USGS topo	15′ series, Silver Lake, Leek Spring Hill; 7.5′ series, Tragedy Spring, Leek Spring Hill
Start	Iron Mountain Road, 0.5 mile west of Highway 88 where the road is no longer plowed. Iron Mountain Road is located 7.4 miles northeast of the Bear River Reservoir turnoff and 7.0 miles west of Silver Lake. This road is the turnoff for Iron Mountain Ski Area. It is shown as Silver Lake Road on the 1956 Silver Lake and 1951 Leek Spring Hill 15′ series topos.

With panoramic views in all directions the setting atop Leek Spring Hill is beautiful. This tour might well become more popular than those to Woods Lake if it were not for the snowmobiles which use Iron Mountain Road. Nevertheless, this tour should not be missed.

You can reach the lookout on Leek Spring Hill by the two routes described in this tour. The easiest follows Iron Mountain Road for 1.2 miles and then another road for the remaining distance to the lookout. Snowmobiles frequent the Iron Mountain Road portion only. The more difficult route follows Iron Mountain Road for only 0.5 mile and includes a traverse of Plummer Ridge.

Begin either of the routes by skiing west on Iron Mountain Road. At first the road will drop slightly; where it levels you will pass a road on your left. Ahead begin climbing and at 0.5 mile from the start you will reach the point **(8)** where the more difficult route via Plummer Ridge turns off. If you choose this route see "more difficult route" below.

Easier Route. Continue along Iron Mountain Road. The road will level off as it traverses around the northeast side of Alder Hill. Once past Alder Hill the road drops slightly and very shortly you will encounter a road heading west (left) from Iron Mountain Road **(9)**. This road will be marked with a ski touring marker.

Turn onto this road and follow it for 1.3 miles along the north side of Plummer Ridge until you reach a saddle **(10)** where Plummer Ridge and the road intersect. At this point the more difficult route will join the easier route once again. Also, there is a road which heads south from here to

Highway 88. That road is described in the Leek Spring Hill from Highway 88 tour.

Continue skiing west on the road you have been on for another 1.2 miles to Leek Spring Hill. The terrain along this part of the route is rolling until the final short and easy climb to the summit. Along this section you will pass two roads on your left. Once at the top, if you enjoy telemarking, you will find the ridge to the northeast of the summit and the adjacent bowl great fun.

More Difficult Route. At 0.5 mile from the starting point leave the road and climb steadily west to the summit of Alder Hill **(11)** which is 300' above the road you left behind. The climb is predominantly through trees and the summit is not distinct.

From what appears to be the highest point you should continue skiing west and gradually down along the ridge. Along this section you will see a road cut through the trees. Follow the road as it follows the ridge. At one point the route will become flat and just ahead it will descend down to the road that the easier route follows **(10)**. Continue to the summit of Leek Spring Hill along the easier route.

Igloo construction   *Charlene Grandfield*

Alder Hill Loop

Difficulty	3
Length	6 miles round trip
Elevation	7250/+600, −600 (7250/+850, −850 by Plummer Ridge)
Navigation	Road and marked trail (Road, marked trail and map for Plummer Ridge route)
Time	Most of a day
Season	December through mid-April
USGS topo	15' series, Silver Lake, Leek Spring Hill; 7.5' series, Tragedy Spring, Leek Spring Hill, Peddler Hill, Bear River Reservoir
Start	Iron Mountain Road, 0.5 mile west of Highway 88 where the road is no longer plowed. Iron Mountain Road is located 7.4 miles northeast of the Bear River Reservoir turnoff and 7.0 miles west of Silver Lake. This road is the turnoff for Iron Mountain Ski Area. It is shown as Silver Lake Road on the 1956 Silver Lake and 1951 Leek Spring Hill 15' series topos.

This tour is a loop which either circles Alder Hill or crosses its top. You will also have the opportunity to visit Leek Spring Hill and enjoy its beautiful vistas. Whatever you choose, this is a pleasant tour which allows you to ski most of a day and only retrace a very short section.

The first objective is to reach the saddle **(10)** where Plummer Ridge intersects a road at a point denoted by BM 7290 on the topo. This point is 2.5 miles from the start of the tour. You can reach it by either of the two routes described in the Leek Spring Hill from Iron Mountain Road tour (no. 6). If you desire to visit Leek Spring Hill itself, you should follow that tour for the additional 1.2 miles and 300' of elevation gain necessary to reach it.

At the saddle previously described you will find a road heading south (left). Ski on this road for 1.9 miles as it winds around and descends very gradually. In this section you will cross two drainages and finally encounter a third **(12)**. At this drainage there will be a small road which leaves the main road and heads northeast (left) up the drainage. This road is marked as a ski touring route.

Follow the road up the drainage for almost 0.2 mile to what appears to be a fork. At this fork take the road that heads east (right) and climb for almost 0.2 mile to a saddle **(13)**.

At the saddle several roads intersect. Head northeast on the left-most road which parallels the hillside for 0.2 mile until you cross a creek.

Continue southeast on the road for 0.3 mile until you reach a ridge top **(14)**.

At the ridge you make a 180 degree left turn and head northwest. There will be two roads heading in that direction. Be sure that you take the left one. Continue on this road for 0.4 mile to a clearing.

At the clearing you turn north (right) and follow it for 0.1 mile until you intersect the road you first skied **(15)**. From this intersection ski 0.4 mile east (right) to the starting point.

Steep traverse

8 Mud Lake Loop

MAP 4
PAGE 31

Difficulty	3
Length	6 miles round trip
Elevation	8000/ + 1200, − 1200
Navigation	Map and compass
Time	Full day
Season	December through April
USGS topo	15′ series, Silver Lake
Start	Highway 88, 2.9 miles southwest of the Silver Lake dam, where the highway makes a right angle turn.

This is an interesting tour in a seldom visited area. You will find that the navigation which is required adds a bit of challenge to the tour and the spectacular views from the summit of Peak 8451 are a treat.

According to the map you should be able to follow a road nearly the entire length of the tour. Since this is difficult to do in reality do not depend on the road.

At the starting point, if you find the snow bank on the south side of the highway too high to climb, you will have to walk towards Silver Lake to find a better spot. From wherever you actually start, ski along the highway until you reach several cabins.

Near the cabins you will find what appears to be a road climbing south up a ridge. Follow this road for 0.6 mile to where it passes to the west of the ridge's high point (1).

From where you pass the highpoint, descend to the southeast for 0.6 mile until you reach a saddle (2). The tracks you make in descending to the saddle will be visible later from Peak 8451.

From the saddle head southwest to Mud Lake. If you cannot find the roadbed you should pick a route heading southwest through the trees. After skiing 0.8 miles you will encounter a large clearing. Continue southwest through some trees and find another clearing and Mud Lake (3).

Halfway down Mud Lake and the clearing, locate a gully heading east since you will probably not be able to find the road located there. Ski east and then northeast, climbing where the road should be. Your goal is to reach Peak 8451 (4) which is 1.5 miles from Mud Lake. If you encounter a problem with trees you are probably too low. In this case ski north towards the ridge. Because cornices may be present you should exercise caution all along the north side of the ridge which includes Peak 8451.

From Peak 8451 you will be treated to 360 degrees of spectacular scenery. To the north is Pyramid Peak which overlooks Desolation Valley. To the east you will see Thimble Peak and Round Top, and to the south Mokelumne Peak dominates the skyline.

Locate the spur which heads northwest from Peak 8451. This spur has a distinctive vertical drop to its east. Looking down the spur you have a view of the original saddle (2) with tracks descending to it from the other side.

Ski down the spur to the saddle staying as high as possible. At the saddle pick up your tracks made on the trip in and retrace them to the highway.

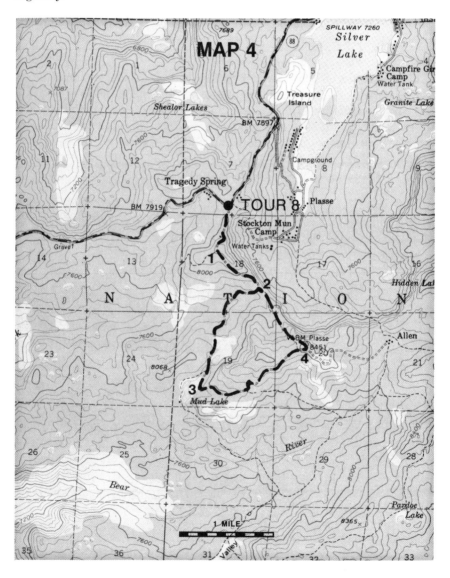

9 Martin Meadow

MAP 5
PAGE 33

Difficulty	1
Length	Short
Elevation	7750/nil
Navigation	Adjacent to plowed road
Time	Short
Season	Late November through April
USGS topo	15′ series, Silver Lake
Start	Highway 88, 2.7 miles north of the Silver Lake dam and 0.7 mile west of the Carson Spur.

This secluded meadow is a delightful location to learn and practice the fundamentals of cross-country skiing.

From the highway, a short gentle downhill glide to the south takes you to the meadow which is surrounded by aspens. You may want to spend part of your time in the meadow and part on the gradual slopes which surround it. Do not attempt to ski the ridge to the east of the meadow since it is subject to blasting and avalanches.

Exploring aspen ringed meadow

Bob Bastasz

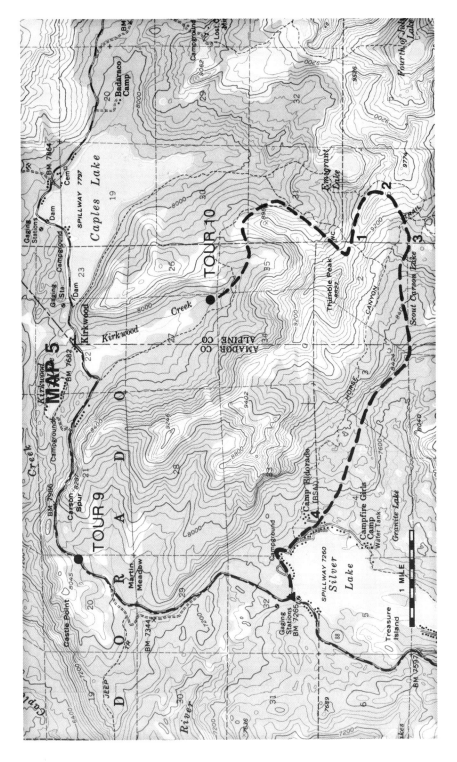

10 Kirkwood to Silver Lake

MAP 5
PAGE 33

Difficulty	4
Length	8 miles one-way
Elevation	7700/+2050, −2500
Navigation	Map and compass
Time	Full day
Season	Late December through April
USGS topo	15′ series, Silver Lake
Start	Main Lodge at Kirkwood Ski Resort off Highway 88, 5.0 miles west of Carson Pass.
End	Silver Lake dam on Highway 88, 4.8 miles west of Kirkwood Meadow.

If you seek the thrill of downhill on cross-country skis, this is an excellent tour for you. From the high point it is a continuous 2200′ descent to Silver Lake. As you descend the 2200′ from the red ridge which separates Kirkwood Meadow from Silver Lake you will be treated to both beauty and challenge. Under ideal conditions no stretch of the descent is excessively steep. If pleasure is your goal, it is highly recommended to do this tour when there is no ice or crust, like a warm spring day.

Start the uphill section of the tour at the Main Lodge at Kirkwood Ski Resort. From there it is a stiff climb to the broad saddle (1) southeast of Thimble Peak and chairlift 4. The easiest route to follow is marked by chairlifts 1, 2, 3 and 4; be sure to stay off the groomed slopes.

As an alternative for reaching the ridge top start the tour at the Kirkwood Ski Touring Center on Highway 88 and follow the Caples-Kirkwood Loop tour (no. 13). That route will lead you to the base of chairlift 4. Although this route will eliminate most of the ski slopes, it will also increase the length of the tour by 2.0 miles.

From the broad saddle to the southeast of Thimble Peak head southeast. Traverse the ridge and pass to the north of its high point. In this section, during most of the winter and spring you will commonly find hard ice and a crevasse paralleling the ridge. Obviously you must exercise a great deal of care in this section.

After rounding the high point you must climb slightly to the south until you reach the ridge again at a saddle (2) just to the northwest of Peak 9774.

Now it is all downhill. Pick your own route heading down to Scout Carson Lake (3). Ski west from Scout Carson Lake and then turn northwest. The terrain is open in most places and as it becomes more level you will encounter small dips which add excitement.

When you reach the cabins at Camp Eldorado which is located adjacent to Silver Lake, you will intersect a road **(4)**. Follow the road to the north and west along the lake until you reach the dam and Highway 88.

Perfect turns   *Kim Grandfield*

11 Caples Lake

MAP 6
PAGE 37

Difficulty	1–2
Length	Up to 7 miles round trip or 4 miles one-way
Elevation	7700/nil
Navigation	Adjacent to plowed road
Time	Few hours to most of a day
Season	Late November through April
USGS topo	15′ series, Silver Lake
Start	Kirkwood Ski Touring Center located on the north side of Highway 88 at Kirkwood Meadow, 4.8 miles east of Silver Lake and 5.0 miles west of Carson Pass.
End	Either the starting point or the turnout on Highway 88 on the south side of the road 0.2 mile east of the highway maintenance station adjacent to Caples Lake.

This tour along the edge of Caples Lake is the closest tour to Kirkwood Meadow for beginners who desire to get off the prepared tracks. If you have mastered the diagonal stride, this tour is an opportunity to experience the rewards of off-track skiing.

From the starting point ski 0.4 mile east along the highway to the western-most dam (1) at Caples Lake. It is not safe to walk on the road in this area because it is often icy and cars can lose control as they make the turn at the dam. From the dam it is easy touring along the southwest side of the lake.

This tour has no particular destination. You should ski as far as desired and then retrace your tracks. As an alternative you can end the tour on the highway at the east end of the lake. Of course you can also begin this tour at the alternate ending point and ski in the opposite direction. No matter what route you take it is never safe to ski on Caples Lake.

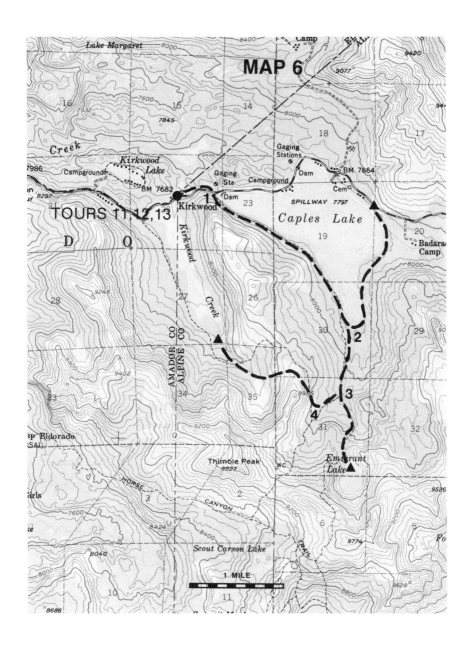

Round Top from Caples Lake

MAP **6**
PAGE 37

Emigrant Lake **12**

Difficulty	3
Length	8 miles round trip
Elevation	7700/ + 900, − 900
Navigation	Map
Time	Full day
Season	Late December through April
USGS topo	15′ series, Silver Lake
Start	Kirkwood Ski Touring Center located on the north side of Highway 88 at Kirkwood Meadow, 4.8 miles east of Silver Lake and 5.0 miles west of Carson Pass.

Emigrant Lake is located in a cirque that is not frequently visited. Here is an opportunity for you to get away from the large number of people which are found elsewhere in the Carson Pass area. The tour to Emigrant Lake is an extension of the previously described Caples Lake tour. Unlike the Caples Lake tour, the tour to Emigrant Lake climbs steadily through dense trees but the climb is not steep.

From the starting point ski 0.4 mile east along the highway to the west-ern-most dam **(1)** at Caples Lake. It is not safe to walk on the road in this area because it is often icy and cars can lose control as they make the turn at the dam.

From the dam continue skiing along the southwest side of the lake. Here you will find the touring easy. You should be aware, though, that it is not safe to ski on the lake because the ice is never stable. After you have skied 2.0 miles along the lake you will reach the southern end **(2)**. Here, at the first creek, you must turn south and ski along its west (right) side into the woods. This creek drains out of Emigrant Lake and you can follow it for the remainder of the distance. Once at the lake do not ski under the steep cliffs.

You can also start this tour at the east end of Caples Lake. In this case the starting point for the tour is near the highway maintenance station the location of which is described in the Caples Lake tour (no. 11). If you choose this route, follow the shore of the lake to its southern end and pick up the route described above. This route is 2.0 miles shorter than the one beginning at the ski touring center.

13 Caples-Kirkwood Loop

MAP 6
PAGE 37

Difficulty	3
Length	6 miles one-way
Elevation	7700/ + 900, − 900
Navigation	Map and compass
Time	Full day
Season	Late December through April
USGS topo	15′ series, Silver Lake
Start	Kirkwood Ski Touring Center located on the north side of Highway 88 at Kirkwood Meadow, 4.8 miles east of Silver Lake and 5.0 miles west of Carson Pass.
End	Main Lodge at Kirkwood Ski Resort off Highway 88, 5.0 miles west of Carson Pass.

Variety is the key word in describing this loop tour, but the distinguishing feature is the downhill run at Kirkwood Ski Resort which completes the loop.

The first half of the tour is along the route to Emigrant Lake. You should refer to the Emigrant Lake tour (no. 12) for details on reaching the southern end of Caples Lake (2).

At the southern end of the lake there are two creeks. You must now follow the western-most creek to the south and into the woods for 0.7 mile. At a place where the terrain to the west of the creek rises more gently than elsewhere (3), turn southwest (right). If you leave the creek too soon you will find yourself climbing quite steeply and will need to traverse farther south.

After you leave the creek, ski 0.3 mile to the edge of the clearing (4) which is the bottom of chairlifts 3 and 4 of Kirkwood Ski Resort.

To get the best run back to Kirkwood Meadow you must climb to the top of chairlift 3. To avoid causing a safety problem do not ski on the groomed slope. From the top of the chairlift you can easily follow the intermediate and then beginner slopes northwest to the main lodge. This is an opportunity for you to test and practice downhill techniques, especially the telemark.

There are two alternatives to this tour which you can consider. The first possibility is to start the tour at the east end of Caples Lake. In this case the starting point for the tour is near the highway maintenance station the location of which is described in the Caples Lake tour (no. 11).

Another possibility is to end the tour at the Kirkwood Ski Touring Center where you started. To do so, you simply ski the length of Kirkwood Meadow. Be aware, though, that the meadow is private property which is leased by the touring center who charges for its use.

Sharing the perfect day

14 Woods Lake from Highway 88

MAP 7
PAGE 42

Difficulty	1
Length	2 miles round trip
Elevation	8300/+100, −100
Navigation	Road and marked trail
Time	Few hours
Season	Late November through April
USGS topo	15' series, Silver Lake
Start	Highway 88, 1.0 mile west of Carson Pass at the turnout on the south side of the highway.

This tour describes the easiest route to Woods Lake which is situated below high mountains. It is a good tour for beginners who want to get away from meadow skiing. If you have a little more experience you will probably enjoy starting the tour from Carson Pass as described in the Woods Lake from Carson Pass tour.

On the south side of the highway adjacent to the starting point you must locate a clearing. Ski down this clearing for 0.1 mile to a road. Since it is in an open area, the road may not be obvious so look for ski tracks on the road. If there are no tracks, look for ribbons which mark the road. In either case, you should make a visual note of this location so that you will recognize it on the return.

At the road turn south (right) and follow it gradually downhill. You will reach a road junction (2) in 0.3 mile but it is not very obvious. If in doubt you should follow the markers.

Take the south (left) fork at the junction and ski on it for 0.6 mile to Woods Lake.

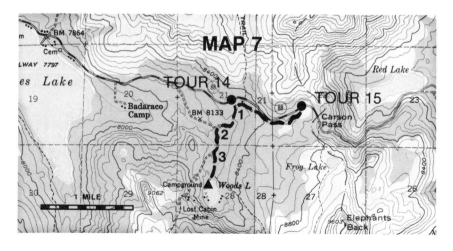

MAP 7
PAGE 42

Woods Lake from Carson Pass 15

Difficulty	2
Length	4 miles round trip
Elevation	8600/ + 400, − 400
Navigation	Road and marked trail
Time	Half day
Season	Late November through April
USGS topo	15′ series, Markleeville, Silver Lake
Start	Highway 88, 0.1 mile west of Carson Pass. Park at the pass and walk or ski to the meadow west of the pass.

For good reason, this tour may well be the most popular one in the Carson Pass area. With only a little experience you will be able to complete this pleasant tour on a snow-covered road to Woods Lake. If you desire an even easier route, you should refer to the Woods Lake from Highway 88 tour. Whichever route you choose, take a lunch and plan to enjoy the afternoon by the frozen lake.

At the starting point, on the west side of the meadow, find a road heading west, gradually downhill and paralleling the highway. Normally this road is well marked by the tracks of other skiers. If you should be lucky enough to hit it immediately after a snowfall or if the tracks seem to head in every which way, you should follow the ribbons which mark the route.

After you have skied 1.2 miles and lost 400′ of elevation, you will reach a road junction (2) which may not be obvious; look for the markers. Turn south (left) at the junction and continue on this road for 0.6 mile to Woods Lake.

As an addition to this tour, you can make a side trip to Lost Cabin Mine. To do so, you must locate the road which intersects the route to Woods Lake 0.3 mile north of the lake (3). Ski southwest up this narrow road for 0.6 mile to the mine. You will find it a challenge to ski the return route with its steep, tight turns.

Ridge above Lost Cabin Mine

MAP **8**
PAGE 45

Winnemucca Lake **16**

Difficulty	3
Length	4 miles round trip
Elevation	8600/ + 400, − 400
Navigation	Map
Time	Half day
Season	December through April
USGS topo	15′ series, Markleeville
Start	Highway 88 at Carson Pass.

This tour to Winnemucca Lake is very popular. You can also use this tour as the start of many other tours in the Carson Pass area. There is, though, one basic drawback to all tours which lead to Winnemucca Lake. Because the west-facing open slopes are often wind-packed they may offer poor touring. Accordingly, you should pick an appropriate time for this tour.

You begin the tour by skiing south and into the woods from the east end of the parking area at Carson Pass. The first 100 yards can be tricky so try not to be discouraged.

After you have skied south for 0.5 mile you will pass Frog Lake **(1)** which is located in a small basin. Continue skiing south and traverse the open slopes on the west side of Elephant Back until you reach Winnemucca Lake which lies in a depression below Round Top.

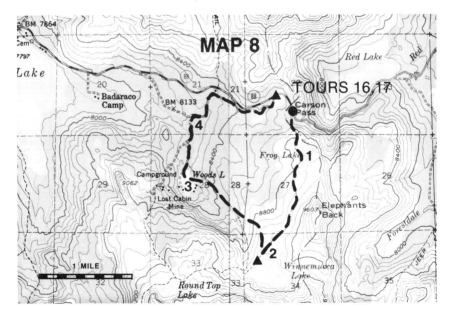

MAP **8**
PAGE 45

17 Winnemucca Lake and Woods Lake Loop

Difficulty	3
Length	5 miles round trip
Elevation	8600/ + 800, − 800
Navigation	Road and map
Time	Most of a day
Season	Late December through April
USGS topo	15′ series, Markleeville, Silver Lake
Start	Highway 88 at Carson Pass.
End	Highway 88, 0.1 mile west of Carson Pass.

This loop trip is pleasant because it allows you to visit both Winnemucca and Woods Lakes without retracing your tracks.

Your first goal is to reach Winnemucca Lake (**2**). Refer to that tour description for details (no. 16).

After reaching Winnemucca Lake, you should ski to Woods Lake (**3**) by following the east (right) side of the creek which connects the two. You should stay as far east and north of the creek as needed to take advantage of the best terrain. Be wary of wind-blown crust or ice which is prevalent in much of this area. Once at Woods Lake you will probably encounter many other ski tourers because of its popularity.

At the north end of Woods Lake you will find a road. Follow it north for 0.6 mile to a junction (**4**). Here, turn east (right) and ski gradually uphill to the meadow located 0.1 mile west of Carson Pass.

Upper Truckee River drainage   *Bob Bastasz*

MAP **9**
PAGE 48

Winnemucca Lake and Lost Cabin Mine Loop **18**

Difficulty	3
Length	6 miles round trip
Elevation	8600/ + 1100, − 1100
Navigation	Road and map
Time	Full day
Season	Late December through April
USGS topo	15′ series, Markleeville, Silver Lake
Start	Highway 88 at Carson Pass.
End	Highway 88, 0.1 mile west of Carson Pass.

This tour has all the features which make it one of my favorites in the Carson Pass area. The loop allows you to cover miles of interesting terrain without retracing your tracks. Much of the route is through open areas which offer beautiful views. Also, part of the trip is in an area which is not frequently traveled.

You start by following the well-traveled route to Winnemucca Lake (no. 16) **(1)** as described separately.

Cross the outlet creek at Winnemucca Lake and climb west up the slope which leads to the low north ridge of Round Top. You will reach Round Top Lake **(2)** just ahead. If it's warm when you start this tour don't be surprised if you need some warmer clothes by the time you reach Round Top Lake as this area is notorious for strong winds. Also, be aware that the steep, crusted slopes can be prime avalanche terrain after new snow has fallen or while other unstable conditions exist.

Once you reach Round Top Lake you will have left most tourers behind and the best skiing is just ahead. Your next objective is to reach a small meadow **(3)** just above and west of Lost Cabin Mine **(4)**. From Round Top Lake ski north towards the east side of a short but very prominent and beautiful ridge which is located just west of the meadow. Be careful of the small cornices which might exist just above the meadow.

Once you reach the meadow, ski to its east side where you will find an obvious route which drops sharply to Lost Cabin Mine **(4)**. The mine is at most 0.1 mile from the meadow.

At the mine you will see a narrow road which heads to the northeast. Follow that road as it descends steeply to Woods Lake Road **(5)** which is usually very well-traveled.

From the junction Woods Lake is located 0.3 mile to the south (right). To return to Carson Pass you should turn north (left) at the junction and ski for 0.3 mile until you reach another junction **(6)**. Here, turn east (right) and climb up the road to Carson Pass.

If you would like a similar but easier tour to the one described here,

47

18

you may wish to consider the Winnemucca Lake and Woods Lake Loop tour.

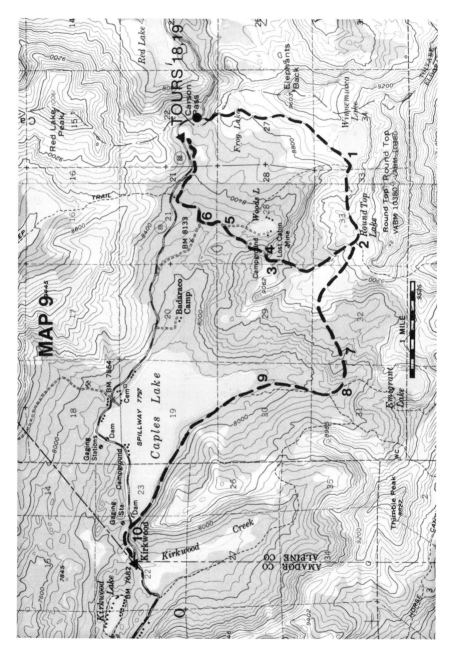

MAP 9
PAGE 48

Carson Pass to Caples Lake

19

Difficulty	4
Length	8 miles one-way
Elevation	8600/ + 700, − 1600
Navigation	Map and compass
Time	Full day
Season	Late December through April
USGS topo	15' series, Markleeville, Silver Lake
Start	Highway 88 at Carson Pass.
End	Kirkwood Ski Touring Center located on the north side of Highway 88 at Kirkwood Meadow, 4.8 miles east of Silver Lake and 5.0 miles west of Carson Pass.

There are a number of interesting tours on the south side of Highway 88 which begin at Carson Pass. This tour, which originates at Carson Pass and terminates at Caples Lake, is by far the most challenging because it covers a wide variety of terrain and requires considerable navigation.

Winnemucca Lake (1) is the first objective and you reach it by following the route described for that tour (no. 16).

At Winnemucca Lake cross the outlet and climb west up the slope which leads to the low north ridge of Round Top. You will reach Round Top Lake (2) just ahead. Ski with caution in the Round Top vicinity where avalanche conditions can exist.

From Round Top Lake ski northwest down easy terrain for 0.5 mile and then turn southwest. As you continue in this direction you will cross a small gully (7). At the gully turn west. You then climb over a small rise before dropping into the Emigrant Lake drainage (8). Emigrant Lake is to the south.

Continue north along the west (left) side of the creek for 1.0 mile until you reach the south end of Caples Lake (9). Next you ski along the southwest shore of Caples Lake for 2.0 miles to a dam and the highway (10). Cross the highway and ski the short distance west to the Kirkwood Ski Touring Center and the end of the tour.

An alternate end for this tour is the east shore of Caples Lake where it meets Highway 88. If you are interested in that variation refer to the Caples Lake tour (no. 11) for details.

20 Meiss Lake

MAP 10
PAGE 52

Difficulty	3
Length	7 miles round trip
Elevation	8600/ + 700, − 700
Navigation	Map
Time	Full day
Season	Mid-December through mid-April
USGS topo	15' series, Markleeville, Silver Lake
Start	Highway 88, 0.1 mile west of Carson Pass. Park at the pass and walk or ski to the meadow west of the pass. The starting point is on the north side of the highway which is across the highway from the meadow.

The tour to Meiss Lake is the start of several longer and more difficult tours including one-way trips to Big Meadow and Echo Summit. Regardless, you will find that Meiss Lake is well worth a trip in its own right. The skiing in the Upper Truckee River drainage is great and the views from above are spectacular.

From the starting point, work your way west for 0.5 mile while climbing gradually. Next, turn to the northwest and climb uphill for 0.5 mile to a broad saddle (1). If the south-facing slopes leading to the saddle are partially barren take off your skis and walk. In this first section of the tour you must take care to avoid the slopes beneath the southwest ridge of Red Lake Peak which may be avalanche prone.

Once you have reached the saddle take a break and enjoy the views. Round Top dominates the horizon to the south. To the north is a view of Lake Tahoe with the Upper Truckee River flowing toward it.

From the saddle ski north staying to the east (right) of the gully you are descending because the ridge to the west (left) is avalanche prone. After descending for 0.8 mile you will reach a meadow (2). At this meadow cross to the east (right) side of the Upper Truckee River and continue north. You will soon pass two old cabins. Ahead 0.8 mile you will reach a large meadow (3) which extends to the north and slightly east. Meiss Lake is at the far end of this meadow.

Snow cave below Round Top   *Charlene Grandfield*

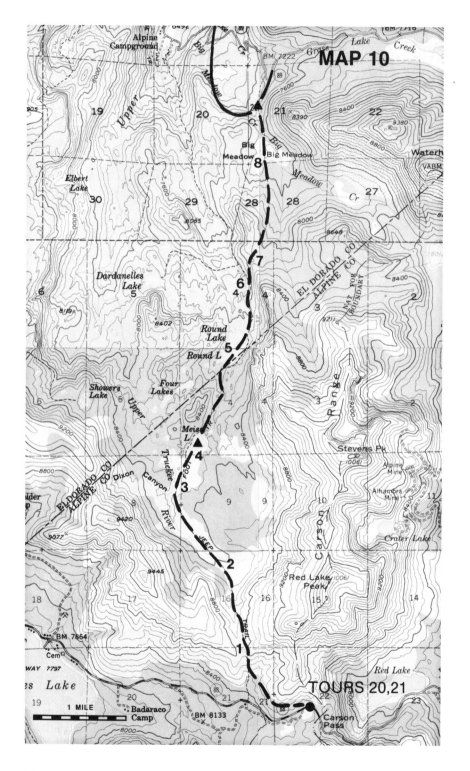

MAP 10

TOURS 20,21

MAP **10**
PAGE 52

**Carson Pass to
Big Meadow**

21

Difficulty	4
Length	8 miles one-way
Elevation	8600/ + 300, − 1600
Navigation	Map and compass
Time	Full day
Season	Late December through mid-April
USGS topo	15′ series, Markleeville, Silver Lake, Fallen Leaf Lake, Freel Peak
Start	Highway 88, 0.1 mile west of Carson Pass. Park at the pass and walk or ski to the meadow west of the pass. The starting point is on the north side of the highway which is across the highway from the meadow.
End	Highway 89 exactly 5.0 miles south from Highway 50 in Meyers. This point is approximately 1.8 miles west of the west end of Grass Lake. There is a turnout on the north side of the road.

This tour combines wide open skiing in the Upper Truckee River drainage and tight downhill terrain in the second half of the tour. A proficiency in winter navigation is a must.

You start this tour by skiing to Meiss Lake **(4)** via the route described separately (no. 20).

From the north end of Meiss Lake follow the outlet creek for 1.0 mile until you reach Round Lake **(5)**. If the snow conditions are poor you may have to pick your way through brush and boulders to reach the lake.

From Round Lake continue north paralleling the ridge which lies to the east, and staying level and close to it. After you pass below a rock outcropping **(6)** start to traverse up the hillside in the fairly open terrain to a saddle **(7)** located in the woods.

Cross the saddle to its east side. Below you will be one of the creeks which feed Big Meadow Creek. You now continue by traversing north paralleling the ridge and drainage. As you traverse you will lose elevation continuously for 1.0 mile until you reach Big Meadow **(8)**.

Ski to the north end of Big Meadow and descend to Highway 89 along Big Meadow Creek. Stay to the east (right) of the creek as you descend.

Route finding between Carson Pass and Echo Summit

MAP 11
PAGE 56

Carson Pass to
Caples Lake Ridge Loop **22**

Difficulty	4
Length	10 miles one-way
Elevation	8600/+900, −1600
Navigation	Map and compass
Time	Full day
Season	Mid-December through mid-April
USGS topo	15′ series, Markleeville, Silver Lake, Fallen Leaf Lake
Start	Highway 88, 0.1 mile west of Carson Pass. Park at the pass and walk or ski to the meadow west of the pass. The starting point is on the north side of the highway which is across the highway from the meadow.
End	Highway 88, 0.2 mile east of the highway maintenance station adjacent to Caples Lake. There is a turnout on the south side of the road.

This tour which circles a ridge is filled with exceptionally fine ski touring terrain which includes wide open bowls and slopes, plus many fine views. All in all, this tour is a gem although much of the terrain is avalanche prone. You will see cornices in many places and should exercise caution.

Begin by following the route to Meiss Lake (no. 20). Just before you reach Meiss Lake cross the Upper Truckee River to the west side **(1)**. Continue northwest along the river and out of the trees for 0.7 mile. When you have gone 0.7 mile (there is no landmark) turn west and climb up a large slope to the top where you will find a flat area. Ski 0.1 mile to the northwest until you reach Showers Lake **(2)**.

From Showers Lake you traverse west and then northwest on a bench below a steep ridge. To the east of the bench will be a steep drop into the Upper Truckee River drainage. At the north end of the bench you continue climbing northwest until the terrain levels off at the north end of the ridge **(3)**.

At the north end of the ridge you turn to the south to return to Highway 88 via the west side of the ridge. You should ski south for 1.8 miles while contouring the ridge. You then drop very steeply for 300′ and turn east to reach Schneider Camp **(4)**.

From Schneider Camp the final run south down to Highway 88 is an easy one on a road. When you reach the maintenance station ski southeast to reach the ending point. In the near future the section from Schneider Camp to the end may be along tracks prepared by Kirkwood Ski Touring Center.

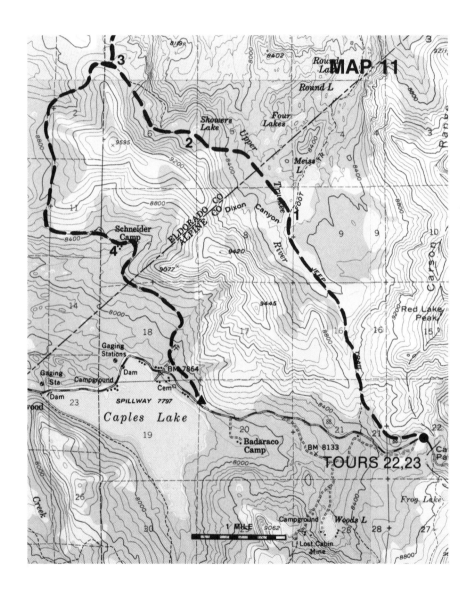

MAP 11

TOURS 22,23

1 MILE

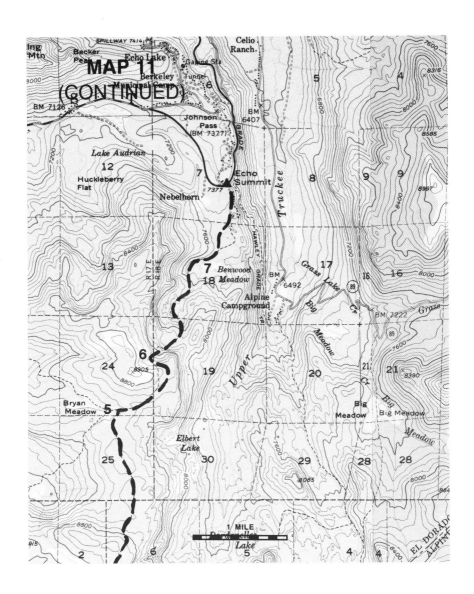

23 Carson Pass to Echo Summit

MAP **11**
PAGES 56–57

Difficulty	4
Length	11 miles one-way
Elevation	8600/+900, −2100
Navigation	Map and compass
Time	Full day
Season	Mid-December through mid-April
USGS topo	15′ series, Markleeville, Silver Lake, Fallen Leaf Lake
Start	Highway 88, 0.1 mile west of Carson Pass. Park at the pass and walk or ski to the meadow west of the pass. The starting point is on the north side of the highway which is across the highway from the meadow.
End	Highway maintenance station located at Echo Summit on Highway 50.

This classic tour between Carson and Echo Passes is great for advanced skiers. The high elevation and excellent terrain will provide you with the opportunity to enjoy beautiful panoramas along the entire tour.

The first half of this tour is identical to the first half of the Carson Pass to Caples Lake Ridge Loop tour (no. 22). Refer to those directions to reach the north end of the ridge (3) where the Carson Pass to Caples Lake Ridge Loop tour turns south. If you wish to ski to Echo Summit continue north instead.

Ski straight north for 2.0 miles to Bryan Meadow (5). As you ski, stretch out and kick up your heels along this enjoyable section.

From Bryan Meadow ski 0.1 mile east to a broad saddle. Continue by contouring to the northeast and then north until you reach the top of a steep gully (6) which is located to the northeast of Peak 8905. Descend the gully carefully as it is avalanche prone. If it is icy you may find it easier to walk down. If necessary stay in the trees alongside the gully.

From the bottom of the gully you ski north following the creek. The creek will lead you to a small meadow and then to Benwood Meadow (7). Continue skiing north through an area with boulders until you reach the cabins at the Summer Home Tract. From the cabins ski to the north for 0.3 mile on a road to Echo Summit.

Snow sculpture

MAP 12
PAGE 61

24 Old Highway 88

Difficulty	2
Length	2 miles one-way
Elevation	8600/ − 800
Navigation	Road
Time	Short
Season	Late November through April
USGS topo	15′ series, Markleeville
Start	Highway 88 at Carson Pass.
End	Red Lake turnout on Highway 88, 2.3 miles east of Carson Pass.

The 1956 Markleeville topo in the vicinity of Carson Pass and Red Lake is incorrect because it shows the old highway. The new one now runs to the north of Red Lake. This tour on Old Highway 88 is entirely downhill.

From the parking area walk east 100 yards to the old roadway on the south side of the highway. Ski down this road for 0.2 miles to an obvious lookout point.

Just before reaching the lookout point there is a monument located about 20 yards to the south of the road. This is a memorial to the unknown pioneers, one of whom is buried here, who brought honor and stability to the character of California. The monument stands only several feet high so your ability to locate it will depend on the snowpack.

Continue down the road to Red Lake. You will probably ski the 1.6 miles of this tour in much less than one hour. You can increase the length of the tour by combining it with a tour towards Forestdale Creek which is described separately. Also, if no shuttle car is available, you will have to trek back up to Carson Pass.

One word of caution. Due to the steepness of the cliff to the south of Old Highway 88 and its orientation to the prevailing wind this route is prone to avalanches. Do not ski here unless you are sure it is safe.

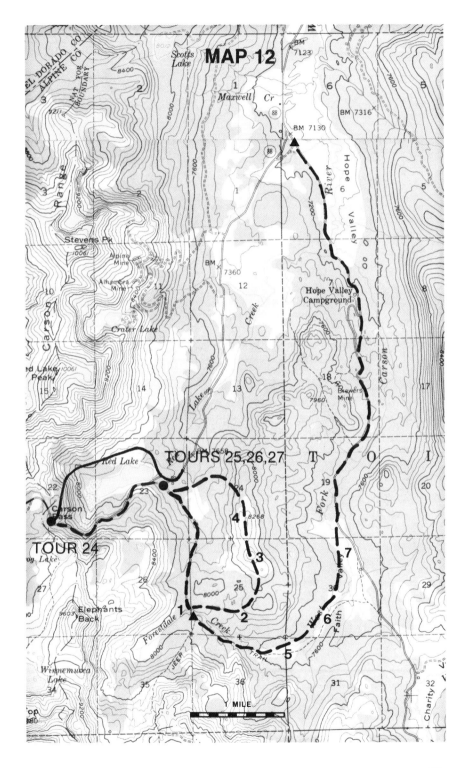

Balloons in Hope Valley   *Bob Bastasz*

MAP **12**
PAGE 61

Forestdale Creek **25**

Difficulty	2
Length	3 miles round trip
Elevation	7800/ + 200, − 200
Navigation	Road and marked trail
Time	Few hours
Season	Late November through April
USGS topo	15′ series, Markleeville
Start	Red Lake turnout on Highway 88, 2.3 miles east of Carson Pass.

For many years this tour to Forestdale Creek was a gem which few people had discovered. Now the secret is out and an ever-increasing number of skiers are enjoying the most rewarding short tour in the Carson Pass area. For the most part the terrain is quite level though there are some ups and downs which might challenge the novice.

From the start ski south on a road. You can ski the entire distance to Forestdale Creek on this road but it is difficult to follow. Fortunately, the route has been marked.

For the first 0.5 mile of the tour there will be a meadow to the east of the route. Past the meadow you will begin climbing very gradually to the south. From the crest of the climb, make a short downhill run to the creek.

Once you have reached Forestdale Creek you can return or continue in one of several directions. You can make a short easy extension of the tour by crossing the creek and following it southwest (right) to a bowl which is the headwaters of Forestdale Creek. Here you will often find ideal snow conditions for telemarking.

If you are an intermediate skier you may enjoy making a loop by returning to the start via Rabbit Ridge if the snow conditions permit.

26 Rabbit Ridge

MAP **12**
PAGE 61

Difficulty	3
Length	4 miles round trip
Elevation	7800/ + 500, − 500
Navigation	Road, marked trail and map
Time	Half day
Season	Late December through March
USGS topo	15′ series, Markleeville
Start	Red Lake turnout on Highway 88, 2.3 miles east of Carson Pass.

Named by locals, Rabbit Ridge is the ridge east of the route to Forestdale Creek. The tour along Rabbit Ridge is an alternate route for returning from Forestdale Creek to the starting point. This route is for strong intermediates who want to get a birds-eye-view of this area.

This tour will treat you to spectacular views from the ridge top where you can familiarize yourself with the lay-of-the-land. You should realize, though, that the ridge is windswept and if there are bare portions you will want to walk along the top. Still the views make it all worthwhile.

Ski to Forestdale Creek (1) as described separately (no. 25). As you descend to the creek along the short final stretch, you will find a road which heads east (left) from the road you are on.

Turn onto this road and ski on it for 0.4 mile to just west of a small knob (2). Here you must leave the road and turn north (left) toward Rabbit Ridge. As you continue north the ridge will become obvious. Continue by ascending to the southern-most high point (3) of the ridge.

Ski or walk along the ridge to Peak 8268 (4). From this peak carefully pick your route down to the north. Beware that these slopes are normally corniced and much of the area is windpacked. Ski north and when you are 0.3 mile from the peak you must locate a fairly obvious route which descends to the west. Ski down this route to more gentle terrain.

The starting point is now west of your location. Ski the final 0.5 mile back through the rolling and sometimes wooded terrain.

Technique for getting a drink

MAP 12
PAGE 61

27 Red Lake to Hope Valley

Difficulty	3
Length	9 miles one-way
Elevation	7800/ + 150, − 850
Navigation	Road and map
Time	Full day
Season	December through mid-April
USGS topo	15′ series, Markleeville
Start	Red Lake turnout on Highway 88, 2.3 miles east of Carson Pass.
End	Junction of Highway 88 and the road to Blue Lakes. The turnoff to Blue Lakes is 6.5 miles east of Carson Pass and 2.5 miles west of Picketts Junction (intersection of Highways 88 and 89). Turn south onto the road that goes to Blue Lakes and park.

This loop tour passes through two beautiful valleys, Hope and Faith. If you are new to navigating without a road or marked trail this tour will also give you a little route finding challenge. Also enticing, of course, is the net elevation loss of 700′.

When you arrive at the ending point of the tour to place a shuttle car, you will probably find the sight and noise of snowmobiles objectionable. Nevertheless, the snowmobiles will not be that unpleasant if you follow two suggestions. First, only ski this tour in the direction described, Red Lake to Hope Valley. Second, plan your tour so that the ending point is reached in the late afternoon; the later the better. If you follow these suggestions you will encounter surprisingly few snowmobiles most of which will be close to the ending point.

From the starting point ski the 1.5 miles to Forestdale Creek (1) as described separately (no. 25). At Forestdale Creek cross the bridge and ski east along the creek for 0.8 mile to a clearing (5). This clearing is the first of three which form Faith Valley. Depending on the snow conditions you may choose to recross the creek in this section between the bridge and the clearing.

When you reach the clearing cross Forestdale Creek to the north side if you have not already done so. Ski to the east end of this clearing. At its end, ski through some trees to the second clearing (6). Here, Forestdale Creek enters the West Fork of the Carson River which flows to Hope Valley.

Ski the length of the second clearing. At its end, again ski through some trees to the third and largest of the clearings which comprise Faith Valley (7). Where you intersect the third clearing will be determined by the route you pick through the trees.

From the topo map you will see that the route you have skied along Forestdale Creek and the West Fork of the Carson River leaves you headed north with Blue Lakes Road on the east side Faith Valley. Ski north through the valley and locate the road at the north end.

Follow the road north for 4.5 miles to Hope Valley and the end of the tour. You will probably find the road well-packed by snowmobiles and the skiing will be fast with a few long downhill stretches.

Hope Valley

Horse Meadow

MAP **13**
PAGE 71

Red Lake to Grovers Hot Springs **28**

Difficulty	5
Length	10 miles one-way
Elevation	7800/ + 450, − 2350
Navigation	Road and map
Time	Very long day
Season	February through early April
USGS topo	15′ series, Markleeville
Start	Red Lake turnout on Highway 88, 2.3 miles east of Carson Pass.
End	Grovers Hot Springs State Park, 3.5 miles west of Markleeville on Hot Springs Road. Park either at the hot springs or at the campground depending on the exact termination point chosen.

The appeal of this tour may be the physical challenge or the enticement of a soak in the hot springs at the end. Regardless, given all the other excellent tours in the Carson Pass area, why people choose this tour is a mystery to me.

While you may find this tour passable as early as January in an early snowfall year, I highly recommend doing this tour late in the season and better still in an extra high snowfall year because the quality of the skiing along the lower reaches of Charity Valley Creek depends almost solely on the snow depth. You should be prepared to ski in the very narrow canyon filled with boulders, vertical drops and lots of brush. Even when conditions are good you will probably have to take off your skis and walk either in the difficult section or as you approach Hot Springs Valley where the snow disappears.

Whatever the season, survey the avalanche danger before attempting this tour and remember to bring a bathing suit and money for admission to the state park facility.

Ski the 1.5 miles from the starting point to Forestdale Creek (**1**) as described separately (no. 25). Here, you should cross to the south side of the creek and find a route heading east along it. Ski east until you reach a clearing (**2**). In the section between the bridge and the clearing you may find it advantageous to recross the creek occasionally depending on conditions. This clearing is the first of three which comprise Faith Valley.

From the east end of the first clearing ski northeast through the trees to the second clearing. From the northeast end of this second clearing ski east through the trees to the third clearing and find Blue Lakes Road on its east side (**3**). The road will probably be well-tracked by snowmobiles.

28

While following this road south (right) towards Blue Lakes for 0.8 mile, you will climb 300′ to a saddle **(4)** where the road levels off and Charity Valley begins. You will see the ruins of a settler's cabin at the edge of the valley.

At the cabin, you should leave the road and follow the summer trail for 3.5 miles northeast along Charity Valley Creek to Hot Springs Creek **(5)**. The skiing for the first 1.5 miles along Charity Valley Creek will be easy but past here the canyon closes in and the difficulty increases dramatically. The skiing will be very slow for the last 2.0 miles so it is important that you plan to reach this point early.

When you reach Hot Springs Creek cross to its northeast side and descend to the east along a route which stays well to the north of the creek. This is where the new summer trail is located and avoids the major obstacles which exist along the trail shown on the 1956 topo.

Hot Springs Valley and the buildings located at the hot springs will become visible as you descend. When you reach the valley head for the hot springs. The shortest route will require you to ford the creek. As an alternative parallel the creek until you reach the campground at Grovers Hot Springs State Park and cross a bridge. The additional distance is 0.5 mile.

Hope Valley   *Bob Bastasz*

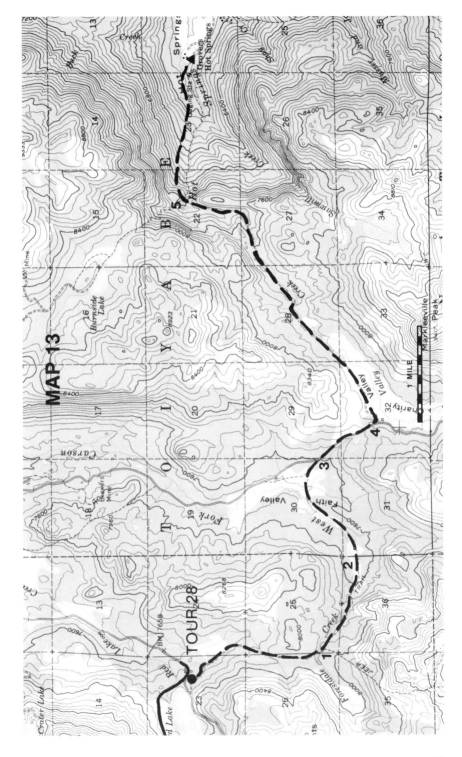

MAP 13

TOUR 28

71

29 Red Lake to Lake Alpine

MAP 14
PAGES 74–75

Difficulty	5
Length	23 miles one-way
Elevation	7800/ + 2600, − 2850
Navigation	Road, map and compass
Time	One very long day or two days
Season	January through mid-April
USGS topo	15′ series, Markleeville, Dardanelles Cone, Big Meadow
Start	Red Lake turnout on Highway 88, 2.3 miles east of Carson Pass.
End	Highway 4, 2.5 miles east of Bear Valley where the road is no longer plowed.

The challenging and scenic tour from Red Lake to Lake Alpine is chuck-full of perfect ski touring terrain for advanced skiers. Completing this tour in one day requires a great deal of stamina, many hours of daylight and good snow conditions. If you choose to take two days to complete this tour, as is normally done, you will find many ideal places to camp along the way.

Ski to Forestdale Creek (1) following the route described separately (no. 25). You cross the creek on a bridge and continue on a jeep road which heads southwest up through the trees. This road will be barely visible and will disappear altogether as the trees get sparse. Continue by skiing south in the open terrain to a broad saddle which is often referred to as Forestdale Pass (2). To the west of the pass is the headwaters of Forestdale Creek.

From Forestdale Pass traverse south through the trees to the next saddle south (3). If you can find the road shown on the topo you can follow it part of the way to the saddle. If not, make sure that the route you pick does not drop below the saddle because that will cause you to head down into Summit City Creek which is the wrong direction.

From the saddle continue southeast to Upper Blue Lake (4) and then to Lower Blue Lake (5). This section between the lakes is a pleasant change from the ups and downs of the previous miles. If you take two days for this tour there will be time to enjoy the serenity of these large and beautiful lake basins. Depending on the season you may or may not find it safe to ski on the lakes themselves.

Near the dam at the south end of the lower lake are several buildings and the end of the road from Hope Valley. From the dam ski south along Blue Creek for 1.0 mile until you reach Clover Valley. This section along Blue Creek is heavily wooded and the skiing is easiest adjacent to the creek which will probably have cut an impressive groove into the snow as it winds down the valley. Secluded Clover Valley is a delightful place to spend the night.

From Clover Valley continue by skiing south for 0.5 mile until you encounter a narrow spot which, depending on conditions, you should negotiate by skiing near or above to the west (right) of the creek. From this point ski 0.7 mile to Deer Valley and Deer Creek **(7)**.

The ridge which separates Deer Valley and Highway 4 is your next obstacle. While the 300' elevation gain and 600' loss required to cross the ridge are not overwhelming, you will find the navigation difficult due to heavy woods, few landmarks, and the up and down terrain near the ridge top. Pick your own route over this ridge, using your compass for navigation, and try to intersect Highway 4 where the North Fork of the Mokelumne River crosses it **(8)**. There is a meadow here which should be visible as you descend to the highway.

Once you reach Highway 4 follow it southwest as it climbs 900' to Pacific Grade Summit **(9)**. Continue west on Highway 4. In the next 4.0 miles the road is almost perfectly level and traverses a slope which descends to the North Fork of the Stanislaus River. Along this section you will have views to the south which encompass the entire Dardanelles region. After the level section continue on the highway as it descends to Lake Alpine. This section will be fast if snowmobiles have been over the road. This tour ends 0.8 mile west of Lake Alpine.

Rabbit Ridge

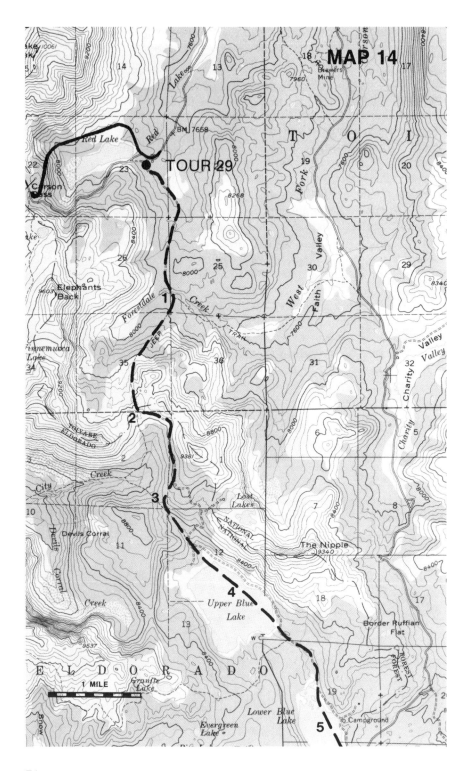

MAP 14

TOUR 29

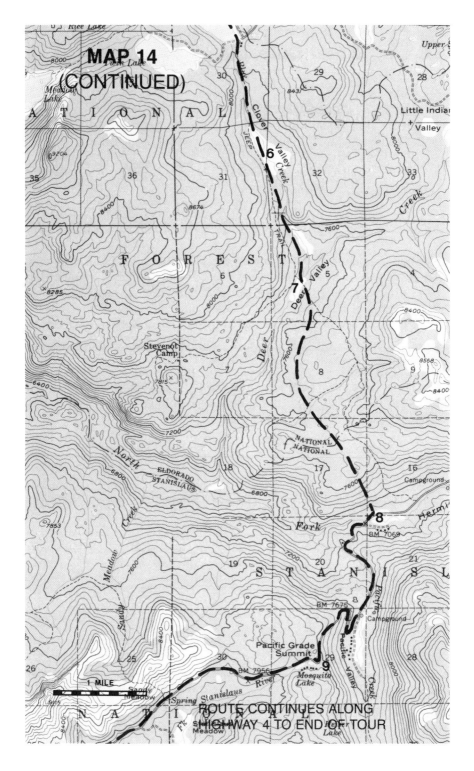

MAP 14
(CONTINUED)

ROUTE CONTINUES ALONG
HIGHWAY 4 TO END OF TOUR

1 MILE

MAP **15**
PAGE 77

30 Crater Lake

Difficulty	3
Length	4 miles round trip
Elevation	7400/+1200, −1200
Navigation	Road and map
Time	Half day
Season	December through April
USGS topo	15′ series, Markleeville
Start	Highway 88, 2.0 miles south of the road to Blue Lakes and 4.8 miles northeast of Carson Pass.

Crater Lake is nestled in a small bowl to the west of Highway 88. You can reach it by a snow-covered road which climbs steeply at times but offers fine views of Hope Valley below. The return trip can offer an excellent downhill run when conditions are good.

Locating the starting point of this tour is not easy. Normally there is an old gate located at the start but it may be removed during the winter so you will have to locate this point by the posts which normally support the gate. To make matters worse, the high embankment blocks the view of the gate posts from the road and the parking is poor at the starting point. The best way to start this tour is to park to the north or south and ski parallel to the highway to the starting point.

Once you have reached the starting point ski northwest on the road. You may find the road difficult to follow as it crosses the flat terrain near the highway but it will become more evident as it climbs. Continue on the road for 1.2 miles until you reach a junction. The north (right) fork heads to points below Stevens Peak. You continue on the south (left) fork toward the bowl where Crater Lake is located which will become more obvious as you proceed.

As you near the bowl do not attempt to climb directly to Crater Lake via the lake drainage because that route is very prone to avalanches. Follow the road which makes a loop south (left) and then west (right), climbing around a high point, to Crater Lake. This last portion is also subject to avalanches so exercise caution.

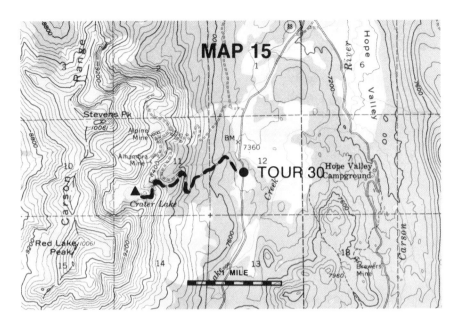

MAP 15

TOUR 30

Break time   *Kathy Tonnessen*

31 Blue Lakes Road

MAP 16
PAGES 80–81

Difficulty	1–4
Length	Up to 23 miles round trip
Elevation	7100/Up to +1500, –1500
Navigation	Road
Time	Up to very long day
Season	December through mid-April
USGS topo	15′ series, Freel Peak, Markleeville
Start	Junction of Highway 88 and the road to Blue Lakes. The turnoff to Blue Lakes is about 6.5 miles east of Carson Pass and 2.5 miles west of Picketts Junction (intersection of Highways 88 and 89). Turn south onto the road that goes to Blue Lakes and park.

The tour on Blue Lakes Road offers an opportunity to visit the beautiful Hope, Faith and Charity Valleys in a single tour. Since the terrain is moderate and the navigation is easy, the difficulty of the tour is determined by the distance you choose to ski.

On weekends the drawback to a tour on Blue Lakes Road is evident when you arrive at the starting point which will be jammed with snowmobilers. Thus mid-week is the only recommended time for a tour here and it is best immediately after it has snowed. If you desire to see this area on the weekend you might be interested in the Red Lake to Hope Valley tour which is described separately. You can also make a loop tour by skiing to Lower Blue Lake via the Red Lake to Lake Alpine tour and returning via Blue Lakes Road.

From the start ski south on Blue Lakes Road. The first 1.5 miles is level as it passes through Hope Valley. From the south end of Hope Valley you climb very gradually for 3.5 miles to Faith Valley (1) and another 1.5 miles to Charity Valley (2). The climb to Charity Valley is steeper than before but still gradual.

South of Charity Valley you continue on the road which climbs to a high point (3). From here it is a very gradual descent to a road junction (4). The fork to the south (left) leads to Tamarack Lake. Continue for 1.0 mile on the fork which heads southwest (right) to Lower Blue Lake. You will find buildings and a dam at the south end of the lake.

Difficulty	1−2
Length	Short
Elevation	7100−7500/nil
Navigation	Adjacent to plowed road
Time	Short
Season	December through mid-April
USGS topo	15′ series, Markleeville, Freel Peak
Start	Park anywhere that is safe and legal along Highway 88 from Picketts Junction (junction of Highways 88 and 89) to 5.0 miles west.

Throughout most of the Hope Valley area there is excellent beginner skiing adjacent to the highway. You will find the easiest terrain in the 2.0 miles closest to Picketts Junction. The entire area offers both flat terrain as well as hills of every size.

Located nearby is the Forestdale Creek tour which is an excellent choice if you are an advancing beginner.

Willow Creek

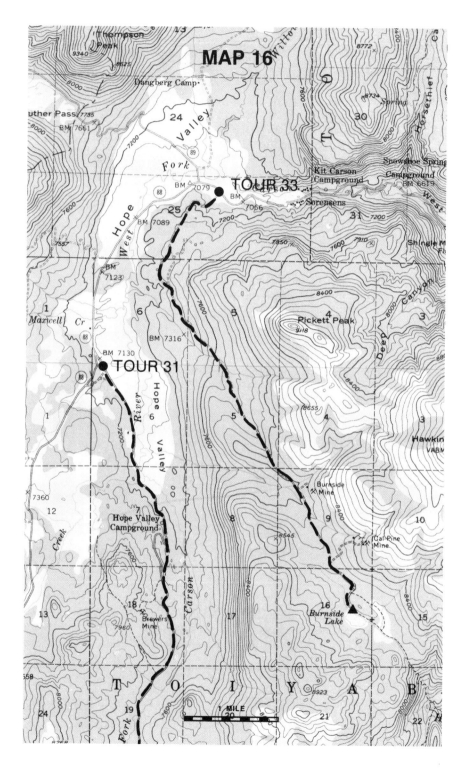

MAP 16

TOUR 33

TOUR 31

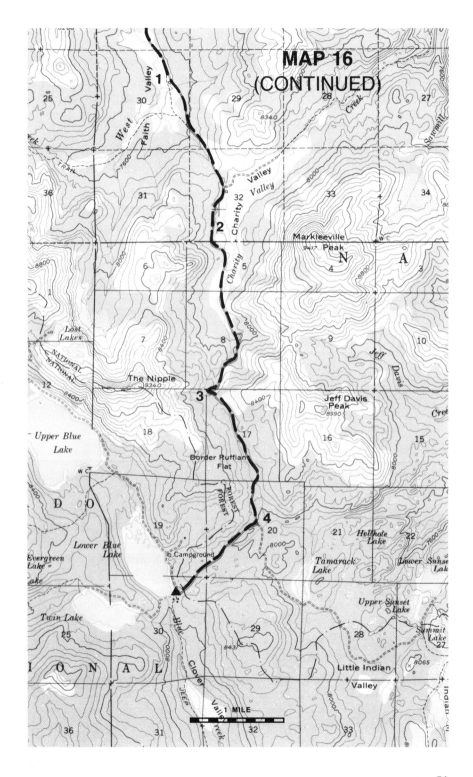

MAP 16
(CONTINUED)

1 MILE

33 Burnside Lake

MAP 16
PAGE 80

Difficulty	3
Length	11 miles round trip
Elevation	7100/+1200, −1200
Navigation	Road
Time	Full day
Season	December through mid-April
USGS topo	15' series, Freel Peak, Markleeville
Start	Picketts Junction (intersection of Highways 88 and 89) in Hope Valley.

When snowmobiles are absent this enjoyable tour offers fine views of Hope Valley and a brisk return trip from Burnside Lake.

The tour begins on the south side of Highway 88 directly opposite Highway 89. Follow the road as it climbs continuously with several steep sections until you reach the high point located 0.6 mile north of Burnside Lake. From here descend slightly to the lake. Along the route you will encounter several junctions. In all cases take the west (right) fork.

If you are interested in more adventure you can ascend Hawkins Peak by departing from the route described at a logged area just southeast of the Cal-Pine Mine turnoff. You should be aware that the mines shown on the topos are on private property and open shafts make these areas dangerous.

Old cabin in Hope Valley

MAP **17**
PAGE 84

Horse Meadow **34**

Difficulty	3
Length	9 miles round trip
Elevation	7450/+1050, −1050
Navigation	Road and map
Time	Full day
Season	December through mid-April
USGS topo	15′ series, Freel Peak
Start	Highway 89, 1.0 mile east of Luther Pass and 1.8 miles north of Picketts Junction (junction of Highways 88 and 89). There is a turnout on the south side of the highway.

This tour is located in a beautiful and peaceful area which is still not popular with ski tourers.

The tour begins on the road located on the north side of the highway. Ski northeast on this road for 2.0 miles until you reach a relatively flat open area **(1)** near and above Willow Creek. Beyond this point it will be difficult to follow the road.

Continue north for 1.4 miles, paralleling the creek and climbing slightly, to where Willow Creek branches **(2)**. Follow the north (left) branch for 0.9 mile to the meadow.

Waxing

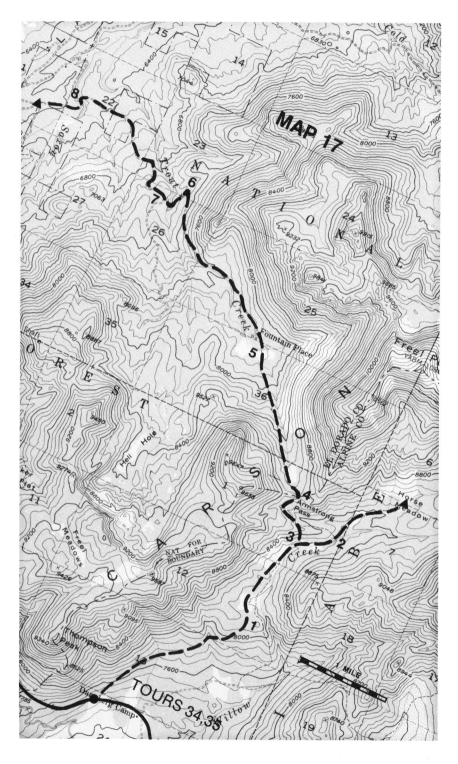

MAP 17

TOURS 34,35

MAP **17**
PAGE 84

Hope Valley to Meyers **35**

Difficulty	4
Length	10 miles one-way
Elevation	7450/ + 1250, − 2400
Navigation	Road, map and compass
Time	Full day
Season	Late December through mid-April
USGS topo	15' series, Freel Peak
Start	Highway 89, 1.0 mile east of Luther Pass and 1.8 miles north of Picketts Junction (junction of Highways 88 and 89). There is a turnout on the south side of the highway.
End	Corner of Oneidas Street and Chibcha in Meyers. From Highway 50 in Meyers follow Pioneer Trail northeast for 1.0 mile. Turn right onto Oneidas Street. Chibcha is 0.2 mile ahead.

This delightful advanced-intermediate tour offers the challenge of finding the route over Armstrong Pass and the descent of the Trout Creek drainage. The scenery is excellent and you should find yourself alone for most of the tour.

The tour begins on the road located on the north side of the highway. Ski northeast on this road for 2.0 miles until you reach a relatively flat open area (1) near and above Willow Creek. Continue north for 1.0 mile, paralleling the creek and climbing slightly, until you reach a point just to the south of Armstrong Pass (3).

Now, leave Willow Creek and climb north to the wide and flat saddle of Armstrong Pass (4). The saddle is covered by trees but you will recognize it as the low point between Peaks 9638 and 10,562.

Cross Armstrong Pass and follow the Trout Creek drainage to the northwest. As you descend the creek the skiing is in general easier on the southwest (left) side though you may find yourself crossing back and forth. Be cautious when crossing on snow bridges.

After skiing 1.5 miles from Armstrong Pass you will reach a large meadow (5). Cross Trout Creek to its northeast side, cross the meadow, and you have reached Fountain Place.

Because the road at Fountain Place is located in dense trees you may not find it immediately. If you have trouble doing so, the easiest solution is to continue skiing along and parallel to Trout Creek. After a short distance turn to the northeast (right) and ski perpendicular to the creek until you intersect the road.

From Fountain Place ski northwest on the road for 0.9 mile. In the next

35

0.9 mile the road will drop sharply so exercise caution after heavy snow-falls and when other avalanche conditions may exist.

Descend until you make a 180 degree turn **(6)** to the left. Past the turn the road starts to level and in 0.3 mile you cross Trout Creek on a bridge. You will reach a road junction **(7)** 0.1 mile ahead.

At the road junction you continue on the road which heads northwest (right) for 1.5 miles until you reach Saxon Creek **(8)**. After crossing on a bridge turn south (left) and follow the road as it turns west. It is 0.3 mile to the end of the tour.

Ridge between Mt. Reba and Cabbage Patch

Bear Valley

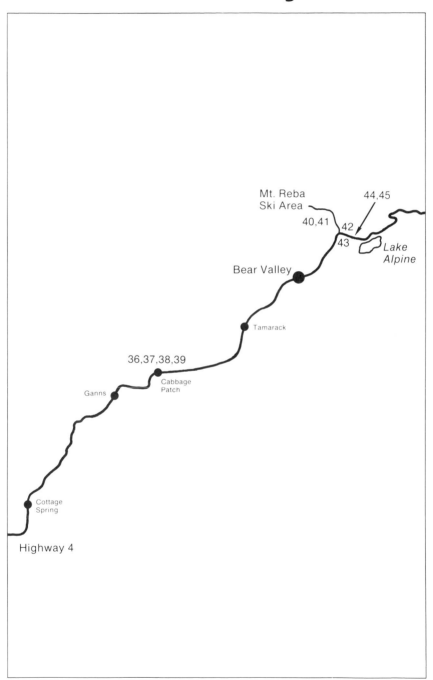

Mt. Reba
Ski Area

44,45

40,41

42

43

Lake
Alpine

Bear Valley

Tamarack

36,37,38,39

Cabbage
Patch

Ganns

Cottage
Spring

Highway 4

36 Mattley Road

MAP **18**
PAGE 91

Difficulty	2
Length	5 miles round trip
Elevation	6700/ + 600, − 600
Navigation	Road
Time	Half day
Season	December through mid-April
USGS topo	15′ series, Big Meadow; 7.5′ series, Calaveras Dome, Tamarack
Start	Junction of Cabbage Patch Road and Highway 4, 0.2 mile west of the highway maintenance station. The maintenance station is 4.0 miles west of Tamarack Lodge. Due to the small parking area it may be necessary to park near the maintenance station.

This pleasant tour on Cabbage Patch and Mattley Roads climbs gradually but continuously up to its highest point. When conditions are good, advancing beginners will find the return descent exciting.

On the north side of the highway follow Cabbage Patch Road which immediately makes a sharp right turn to the northeast. At 0.4 mile you will pass a road on your left **(1)** and after an additional 0.4 mile you will reach another road junction **(2)**. A sign may be visible which indicates "Cuneo" to the left. The fork to the northeast (straight) continues to Thompson Meadow.

Turn west (left) and continue on Cabbage Patch Road for 0.2 mile until you reach a Y **(3)** in the road. You take the fork to the northwest (right) and after traveling another 0.3 mile the road will crest **(4)**. At this point you will see Mattley Road heading east (right) from Cabbage Patch Road. Follow Mattley Road for 0.9 mile to its highest point. This point is the destination of this tour.

For an extension of this tour see the Mattley Ridge tour. As an alternative you can also pass Mattley Road and continue on Cabbage Patch Road as far as desired.

Exploring new route

Difficulty	3
Length	7 or 9 miles round trip
Elevation	6700/ + 1250, − 1250
Navigation	Road and map
Time	Full day
Season	December through mid-April
USGS topo	15′ series, Big Meadow; 7.5′ series, Calaveras Dome, Tamarack
Start	Junction of Cabbage Patch Road and Highway 4, 0.2 mile west of the highway maintenance station. The maintenance station is 4.0 miles west of Tamarack Lodge. Due to the small parking area it may be necessary to park near the maintenance station.

This tour is an extension of the Mattley Road tour. In this tour you will climb steeply from Mattley Road to the top of Mattley Ridge. The ridge is a good destination if you seek fine views and lots of downhill skiing on the return.

Following the Mattley Road tour (no. 36), ski to the highest point **(5)** on Mattley Road. About 50 yards before the high point, ski northwest where Mattley Ridge Road, a jeep trail, should be located.

Mattley Ridge Road will climb quite steeply at first and after 0.5 mile the terrain will become more open and less steep. After you have skied 1.2 miles from Mattley Road you will encounter an unusual snow survey station **(6)**. Shortly after you pass the station you should ski through some trees to the highest point **(7)** which is the destination of this tour.

In reality it is difficult to discern the highest point along Mattley Ridge because the top is quite level for 0.3 mile. The 15′ series topo shows the high point at the northwest end of the ridge. The 7.5′ series topo shows it at the southeast; so take your pick.

If you complete this tour by retracing your route, the round trip distance is 7 miles. On the descent you will find that the open slopes near the top offer excellent downhill terrain and the steeper slopes near Mattley Road offer more challenge.

There is an alternate route by which the return descent is much more gradual. To follow this route you should first ski to the northwest end **(8)** of the ridge. At this point you must locate and follow a road which heads west through the trees, turns southwest and finally intersects Cabbage Patch Road **(9)** 1.1 miles from the ridge top.

Ski south (left) on Cabbage Patch Road for 2.5 miles until you once again meet Mattley Road **(4)**. Now it is easy to retrace your route back to the start. Using this alternate return route makes the tour 9 miles in length.

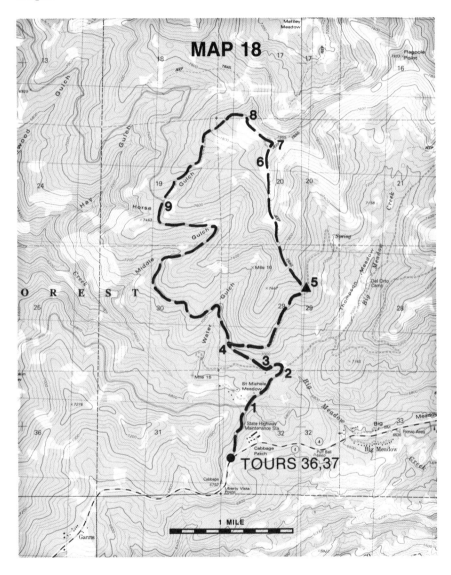

38 Thompson Meadow

MAP 19
PAGE 94

Difficulty	2
Length	4 miles round trip
Elevation	6700/ + 300, − 300
Navigation	Road
Time	Few hours
Season	December through mid-April
USGS topo	15′ series, Big Meadow; 7.5′ series, Calaveras Dome, Tamarack
Start	Junction of Cabbage Patch Road and Highway 4, 0.2 mile west of the highway maintenance station. The maintenance station is 4.0 miles west of Tamarack Lodge. Due to the small parking area it may be necessary to park near the maintenance station.

The tour to Thompson Meadow is an excellent choice for beginners who have mastered the basics. Advancing beginners can also consider the Mattley Road tour.

On the north side of the highway follow Cabbage Patch Road which immediately makes a sharp right turn. After passing roads on your left at 0.4 mile **(1)** and 0.8 mile **(2)** continue to the northeast for another 0.4 mile until you cross Big Meadow Creek.

Almost immediately after you cross Big Meadow Creek the main road will make a sharp turn to the south (right) **(3)**. Do not make this turn; instead continue to the northeast on a lesser road until you reach Thompson Meadow shortly thereafter. The meadow is more than 0.5 mile long.

MAP **19**
PAGE 94

Ridge Loop **39**

Difficulty	4
Length	11 miles round trip
Elevation	6700/ + 1500, − 1500
Navigation	Road, map and compass
Time	Full day
Season	December through mid-April
USGS topo	15′ series, Big Meadow; 7.5′ series, Calaveras Dome, Tamarack
Start	Junction of Cabbage Patch Road and Highway 4, 0.2 mile west of the highway maintenance station. The maintenance station is 4.0 miles west of Tamarack Lodge. Due to the small parking area it may be necessary to park near the maintenance station.

This tour offers spectacular views from the ridge tops and a variety of terrain including mild slopes, steady climbing, traversing ridges and a descent through trees. This tour covers about half of the Mt. Reba to Cabbage Patch tour and does not require a shuttle car, but there is an additional elevation gain.

Refer to the Thompson Meadow tour (no. 38) for directions to Big Meadow Creek. Almost immediately after crossing the creek the main road makes a sharp turn south (right) (**3**). The lesser road to the northeast goes to Thompson Meadow.

Turn south and continue on the main road which climbs steadily for 0.3 mile until you reach a level section. Continue east on the road for 0.4 mile to where it makes a sharp, almost 180 degree turn to the left (**4**), and then starts to climb again. You should continue on this road which climbs, drops and then climbs again as it traverses along the northwest side of a distinct ridge and then eventually reaches the ridge (**5**).

Once you have reached the ridge follow it northeast. You will drop to a saddle and then ascend to a point 0.2 mile east of Peak 7873 (**6**). Here the route you have been skiing intersects the Mt. Reba to Cabbage Patch tour. You are now almost at the halfway point. Although the return trip route is not as straightforward to follow, the trip is less time-consuming because most of the route is downhill or along ridges.

Continue by skiing west toward Peak 7873 and pass this peak to its south. Now head for Flagpole Point (**7**). Do not ascend Flagpole Point; instead, from its south side head southwest along a ridge to Mattley Ridge (**8**). The last short climb to Mattley Ridge is through dense trees.

When you have reached the top of Mattley Ridge ski south through some trees and then south along the ridge through a clearing. Very close

39

to the top of the ridge you will pass a snow survey station. Continuing south from the survey station it is a pleasant gradual downhill run through the clearing. Eventually you will be forced into the trees and the route will descend more steeply. Your objective should be to intersect Mattley Road **(9)**.

Once you are on Mattley Road follow it southwest (right) to Cabbage Patch Road **(10)**. Turn southeast (left) here and ski for 0.5 mile until you reach a junction **(2)**. At the junction turn southwest (right). You are still on Cabbage Patch Road and it leads to Highway 4.

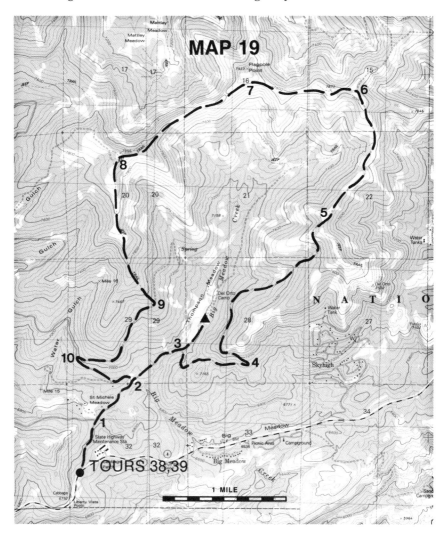

Foul weather skier   *Gary Clark*

40 Mt. Reba to Bear Valley

MAP 20
PAGE 98

Difficulty	4
Length	Up to 7 miles one-way
Elevation	8000/Up to + 1000, − 1900
Navigation	Road and map
Time	Up to most of a day
Season	December through April
USGS topo	15' series, Big Meadow; 7.5' series, Tamarack
Start	Maintenance station located at the high point on the road to the Mt. Reba Ski Lodge. This point is 1.3 miles from Highway 4 and 0.9 mile from the ski lodge.
End	Bear Valley Lodge.

Spectacular views from the ridges and challenging terrain for advancing intermediate skiers are featured in this tour. This one-way tour with 900' of net elevation loss can be accomplished with only one vehicle by making use of the Bear Valley shuttle bus. To do so, leave your car at the lodge where the tour ends and the shuttle bus leaves. The bus will take you to the lodge at the ski area where you can use the parking area shuttle to get to the start of the tour.

The actual distance from the starting point to the ending point of the tour is only 4.3 miles with an elevation change of + 500' and − 1400'. If you wish to find some solitude away from the ski resort you can add a 2 to 3 mile extension. Skiers who are more ambitious might also consider the one-way tour from Mt. Reba to Cabbage Patch. It, too, starts at the ski resort but offers more solitude as it makes one giant traverse to the southwest.

From the main road walk a short distance south to the maintenance station where you begin skiing on a packed road. After you have skied 0.1 mile from the maintenance station you will reach a junction. Make a sharp turn to the south (left) and continue on the road. This road is used by downhill skiers so ski along the edge.

Follow the road as it traverses a ridge and climbs gradually to the summit of Peak 8502 (1). The summit is easy to recognize with its chairlifts, buildings and many downhill skiers. You can also reach this point by riding the Bear or Kuma chairlifts from the ski lodge. Presently the ski resort offers free chairlift rides between 9 and 10 a.m. Taking the lift saves 1.2 miles and 500' of elevation.

At the summit of Peak 8502 locate the Bear Boogie ski run. Slowly descend on it to the southwest. Continue to where the ski run turns northwest and starts to drop steeply. At this point you leave the ski run, cross the ski area boundary, and continue southwest. Make sure that no downhill skiers follow you.

In a very short distance you will reach a prominent point **(2)** where the terrain drops steeply. To the south is Bloods Ridge and you may see a sign indicating that this is the direction of the Bear Valley Trail which is the most direct route to Bear Valley and the end of the tour.

If instead of heading directly to Bear Valley you want to get away from the ski resort environment, continue skiing southwest until you reach the saddle **(3)** above Grouse Valley.

From the saddle ski west ascending a ridge for 0.5 mile to a high point **(4)**. From this location there are spectacular views in all directions. You can also ski another 0.9 mile to the north along a ridge which offers many more vistas. In doing so, be cautious of the steep cliffs to the east which may be corniced.

No matter how far you choose to ski along the ridge, the route to Bear Valley descends along Bloods Ridge; thus it is necessary to backtrack. Ski back to the saddle **(3)** and then traverse east into a bowl and then south in order to intersect Bloods Ridge **(5)**. If avalanche conditions exist, avoid this bowl by skiing back to the previously described prominent point **(2)** and then descend to Bloods Ridge **(5)**.

Once you are on Bloods Ridge ski south along it. There are several places along the ridge where you can descend to Bear Valley. You should look for the cabins located just below the ridge to the east. The snow-covered roads to these cabins provide the easiest route for descending.

It is also possible to ski to the very south end **(6)** of Bloods Ridge where it drops abruptly to Bear Valley below. If you choose to do so, descend to the east (left) until you reach a water tank. There is a road directly below the tank.

Whichever of the routes you choose to Bear Valley, avoid any treeless bowls to the east of Bloods Ridge which might be avalanche prone. You may also encounter very icy conditions along parts of the wind-blown ridge.

Once you have reached a snow-covered road ski a quick 1.5 miles down to the Bear Valley Lodge. Since there are many roads in this area, the best advice is to always head downhill and eventually you will reach the lodge.

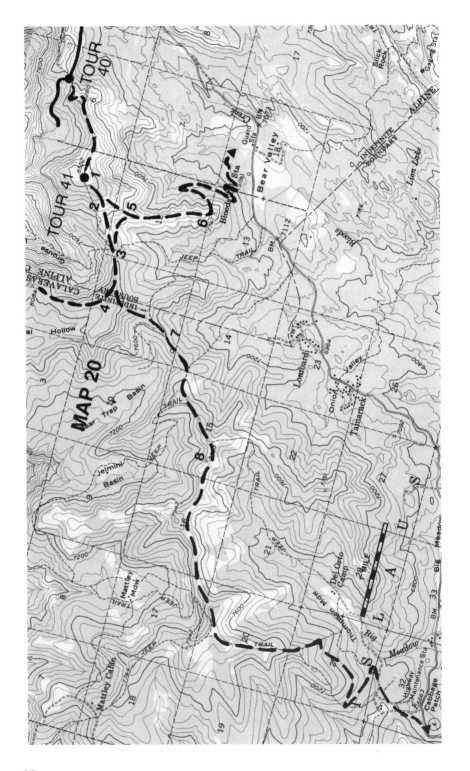

MAP 20
PAGE 98

Mt. Reba to
Cabbage Patch

41

Difficulty	4
Length	9 miles one-way
Elevation	8500/+400, −2200
Navigation	Road, map and compass
Time	Full day
Season	December through mid-April
USGS topo	15′ series, Big Meadow; 7.5′ series, Tamarack, Calaveras Dome
Start	Mt. Reba Ski Lodge
End	Junction of Cabbage Patch Road and Highway 4, 0.2 mile west of the highway maintenance station. The maintenance station is 4.0 miles west of Tamarack Lodge. Due to the small parking area it may be necessary to park near the maintenance station.

If there is a classic tour in the Bear Valley area it is this ski along the high ridges. The actual start of this tour is the summit of Peak 8502 and the route traverses more than 6 miles of ridges. While some of the route is in trees, most is through sparsely wooded and wide open terrain, and thus the views are spectacular. To fully enjoy this tour and for safety you should save it for a fair weather day.

Another selling point of this tour is the more than 2000′ of elevation loss with only a small gain, provided you get to the summit of Peak 8502 by a means other than skiing. Presently the ski resort offers free chairlift rides between 9 and 10 a.m. Both the Bear and Kuma chairlifts go to the summit. If you choose to ski to the summit follow the route described in the Mt. Reba to Bear Valley tour (no. 40) which involves an additional 1.2 miles and 500′ of elevation gain.

At the summit of Peak 8502 locate the Bear Boogie ski run. Gradually descend on it to the southwest. Continue to where the ski run turns northwest and starts to drop steeply. At this point leave the ski run, cross the ski area boundary, and continue skiing southwest. Make sure that no downhill skiers follow you.

Your course to the southwest will take you to the saddle (3) above Grouse Valley. Do not confuse the ridge on which this saddle is located with Bloods Ridge which is located to the south.

From the saddle climb west along the ridge. You should pass to the south of a high point (4) and then descend steeply to the south. Continue to descend to the saddle (7) above Bear Trap Basin. It may be tempting to make a direct traverse between the saddle (3) above Grouse Valley and the saddle (7) above Bear Trap Basin. If you do so you will have to

41

negotiate some densely wooded terrain.

Ski southwest along the ridge toward Peak 7853 **(8)**. A short distance east of the peak you will encounter a clearing which extends south from the ridge. At this clearing you intersect the Ridge Loop tour.

You can reach the ending point for this tour by following the Ridge Loop tour in either direction. The classic route continues west along the ridge and eventually intersects Mattley Ridge before descending. Refer to the Ridge Loop tour (no. 39) for details.

Rime

MAP 21
PAGE 102

Mt. Reba **42**

Difficulty	4
Length	6 miles round trip
Elevation	7600/+1200, −1200
Navigation	Map
Time	Full day
Season	December through April
USGS topo	15′ series, Big Meadow, Silver Lake; 7.5′ series, Tamarack, Mokelumne Peak
Start	Highway 4, 0.1 mile east of Mt. Reba turnoff.

The route to the summit of Mt. Reba climbs steadily over excellent touring terrain. From the moment you leave the road behind, the surrounding area opens up before your eyes. The trees quickly vanish and the route meanders along barren ridges.

Once on the summit of Mt. Reba the views form a 360 degree panorama. On the horizon to the north Thimble Peak, Round Top and Elephants Back mark the Carson Pass area. To the southeast the red volcanic region of the Dardanelles forms a beautiful contrast against a white background. To the west the narrow canyon cut by the North Fork of the Mokelumne River flows into Salt Springs Reservoir, and beyond, on a clear day, you may see Mt. Diablo. Of course to the east is the Sierra crest.

In addition to the scenery, the area in which this tour is located offers excellent slopes for the telemark enthusiast.

From the highway begin by skiing northeast. Very soon you will find yourself on a ridge. After skiing 0.7 mile from the highway you turn north, continue along the ridge toward Peak 8323 **(1)** and pass to the west (left) of that summit. The ridge you are on intersects another ridge **(2)** 0.3 mile to the north. From this intersection you can see Mt. Reba to the northwest.

From the intersection of the two ridges, traverse along the northwest side of the ridge at which you have just arrived, to a distinctive saddle **(3)** located to the northeast. From here gradually climb and traverse northwest to the ridge of which Mt. Reba is a part. Once on this ridge ski west to reach the summit.

While this tour is predominantly along ridges there are several places where you must cross slopes which are avalanche prone. Also, cornices may be present along the leeward side of the ridges, so exercise caution.

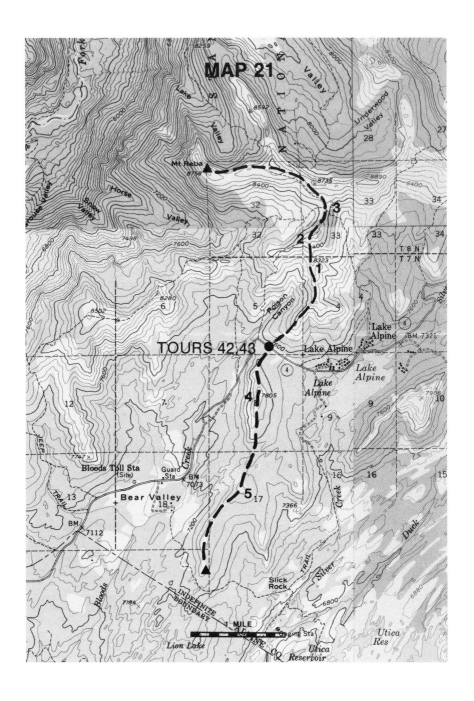

MAP 21

TOURS 42,43

MAP 21
PAGE 102

Osborn Hill and Ridge **43**

Difficulty	3
Length	Up to 5 miles round trip
Elevation	7600/Up to +1100, −1100
Navigation	Map
Time	Up to most of a day
Season	December through April
USGS topo	15' series, Big Meadow; 7.5' series, Tamarack
Start	Highway 4, 0.1 mile east of Mt. Reba turnoff.

This tour is filled with numerous ups and downs, and vistas as it traverses broad ridges. Except for the area immediately in the vicinity of the starting point this tour offers plenty of solitude.

From the highway ski south. After passing a restroom which is part of a summer campground, ascend the ridge for 0.2 mile until you reach a water tank. Continue on the ridge for another 0.2 mile to a high point. Make a short descent to the south and enter the trees. Now climb south to the summit of Osborn Hill (**4**).

From Osborn Hill continue south along the ridge through open terrain for 0.5 mile until you encounter a steep section which you descend. After the descent, continue skiing through a partially wooded area until you cross a small knob (**5**).

Continue skiing south in open terrain as far as you desire or until you reach the point where the ridge starts to drop steeply again.

Return to the starting point by retracing your route. As an alternative, you can pick up the Bear Valley Nordic trail at the end of the ridge and descend to Bear Valley. You must then climb back to the starting point or use a shuttle vehicle. Bear Valley Nordic offers a series of groomed trails in this area for which they charge a use fee.

44 Lake Alpine

MAP 22
PAGE 105

Difficulty	1
Length	2 miles round trip
Elevation	7550/ + 250, − 250
Navigation	Road
Time	Few hours
Season	December through April
USGS topo	15' series, Big Meadow, Dardanelles Cone
Start	Highway 4, 2.5 miles east of Bear Valley where the road is no longer plowed.

From the starting point ski on Highway 4 to Lake Alpine. The short tour to the lake is not particularly rewarding since it is usually well-worn by snowmobiles. Fortunately, there are lots of places for you to explore once you reach Lake Alpine. Caution: do not attempt to ski on the lake because it is never stable.

Cabin in Thompson Meadow   *Kim Grandfield*

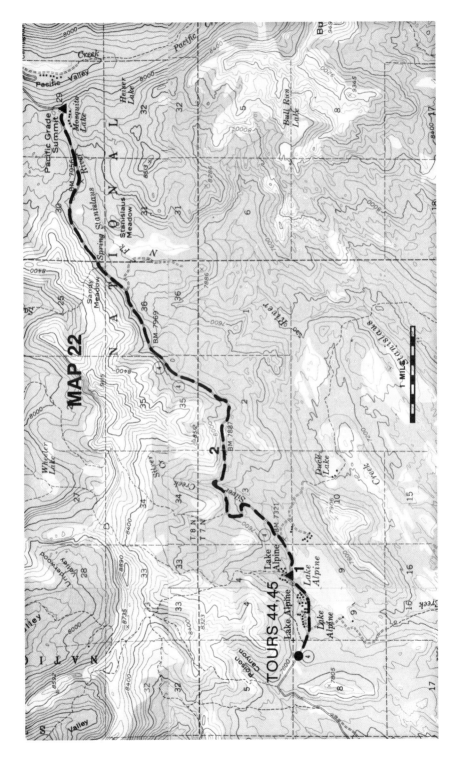

MAP 22

TOURS 44, 45

MAP 22
PAGE 105

45 Pacific Grade Summit

Difficulty	3
Length	14 miles round trip
Elevation	7500/+950, −950
Navigation	Road
Time	Full day
Season	December through April
USGS topo	15' series, Big Meadow, Dardanelles Cone, Markleeville
Start	Highway 4, 2.5 miles east of Bear Valley where the road is no longer plowed.

This tour, which is entirely on Highway 4, may be marred by frequent snowmobilers. However, the highlight of the tour is the view of the Dardanelles area.

Ski on the highway to Lake Alpine (1). Beyond the lake you climb steadily for 1.8 miles to a point near BM 7887 (2). Just ahead the road becomes almost perfectly level and continues level for 4.0 miles until you reach Pacific Grade Summit.

This last 4.0 mile section is a giant traverse of the slope which descends to the North Fork of the Stanislaus River. Along this section you will have views to the south which encompass the entire Dardanelles region.

Corniced ridge

Pinecrest

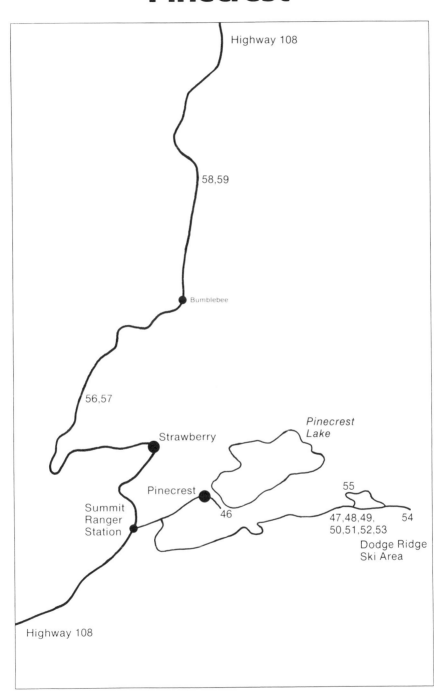

Highway 108

58,59

Bumblebee

56,57

Pinecrest Lake

Strawberry

Pinecrest

55

Summit
Ranger
Station

46

47,48,49,
50,51,52,53

54

Dodge Ridge
Ski Area

Highway 108

46 Pinecrest Lake

MAP 23
PAGE 108

Difficulty	1
Length	Up to 4 miles round trip
Elevation	5600/nil
Navigation	Adjacent to plowed road
Time	Up to half day
Season	January through March
USGS topo	15' series, Pinecrest; 7.5' series, Pinecrest
Start	West end of Pinecrest Lake, 1.0 mile east of Summit Ranger Station.

During the mid-winter months there is often sufficient snow to ski along the south shore of Pinecrest Lake. If you are a beginner you can use the small area in the vicinity of the starting point to get accustomed to your equipment. You can also ski around the lake as far as the inlet creek although other tours in the area normally have better conditions.

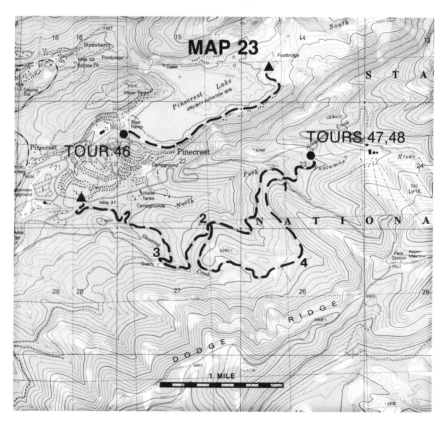

MAP 23
PAGE 108

Crabtree and Sheering Creek Roads **47**

Difficulty	2
Length	4 miles one-way
Elevation	6400/ − 800
Navigation	Road
Time	Half day
Season	Mid-December through March
USGS topo	15′ series, Pinecrest; 7.5′ series, Pinecrest
Start	Dodge Ridge Ski Area Parking loop. Follow Dodge Ridge Road to where it reaches the one-way loop of the ski area parking lot. A right turn at this point leads into the parking area at the Crabtree Trailhead.
End	Dodge Ridge Road opposite Camp Sylvester. This spot is 0.9 mile from Highway 108, 0.2 mile east of Pinecrest School and Meadowview Roads, and 2.5 miles west of the Dodge Ridge Ski Area parking lot.

This enjoyable one-way downhill tour is ideal for advancing beginners; the downhills are very gradual and the route is easy to follow.

From the trailhead ski on the spur road which weaves southwest for 0.4 mile to the intersection with Crabtree Road (**1**). Turn northwest (right) onto Crabtree Road and ski downhill for 1.2 miles to a road junction (**2**).

Continue southwest (right) on Crabtree Road for 0.7 mile to a four-way intersection of roads (**3**). Make a right turn which will turn you around almost 180 degrees and ski down Sheering Creek Road for 1.3 miles until you intersect another road which may be plowed. At the intersection, ski to the northeast (right) for 0.2 mile until you reach the end of the tour.

48 Crabtree Trail Loop

MAP 23
PAGE 108

Difficulty	2
Length	5 miles round trip
Elevation	6400/ + 300, − 300
Navigation	Road and marked trail
Time	Half day
Season	Mid-December through March
USGS topo	15' series, Pinecrest; 7.5' series, Pinecrest
Start	Dodge Ridge Ski Area Parking loop. Follow Dodge Ridge Road to where it reaches the one-way loop of the ski area parking lot. A right turn at this point leads into the parking area at the Crabtree Trailhead.

If you seek a pleasant half day tour in this area, this loop is your best choice. The terrain is easy to negotiate as the route meanders through the trees. Along the route you can make a short detour to Burnt Bowl which is an ideal place for you to enjoy a snack or lunch. This open bowl offers good terrain on which to practice skiing steeper slopes.

From the trailhead ski on the spur road which weaves southwest for 0.4 mile to the intersection with Crabtree Road (1). Cross Crabtree Road and follow the Crabtree Trail signs which are marked with the numeral 1 for 0.8 mile until you reach a small creek which you cross. Just past the creek is a trail junction (4).

From the junction ski to the southeast for 0.2 mile to reach Burnt Bowl. The trail to Burnt Bowl is marked and denoted by the numeral 4. To complete the loop, return to the junction.

From the junction follow the Crabtree Trail markers which head to the west until you intersect a road. Ski west on this road for 1.1 miles to Crabtree Road (2). Turn west (right) onto Crabtree Road and follow it back to the spur road (1). Finally, follow the spur road back to the trailhead.

MAP **24**
PAGE 112

Aspen Meadow **49**

Difficulty	2
Length	4 miles round trip
Elevation	6400/ + 600, − 600
Navigation	Road
Time	Half day
Season	December through mid-April
USGS topo	15′ series, Pinecrest; 7.5′ series, Pinecrest
Start	Dodge Ridge Ski Area Parking loop. Follow Dodge Ridge Road to where it reaches the one-way loop of the ski area parking lot. A right turn at this point leads into the parking area at the Crabtree Trailhead.

Aspen Meadow is a good objective for advancing beginners who want a brisk downhill return.

From the trailhead ski on the spur road which weaves southwest for 0.4 mile to the intersection with Crabtree Road (**1**). Turn southeast (left) and ski up Crabtree Road for 1.1 miles. After making a sharp right turn with the road (**2**), continue for another 0.4 mile and make a left turn with the road (**3**).

Almost immediately after the left turn you will pass a road heading south (right). Stay on Crabtree Road for 0.1 mile until you reach Aspen Meadow and a corral.

Avalanche beacons   *Kim Grandfield*

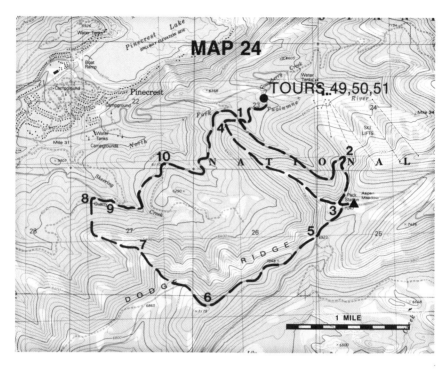

Oops!

MAP 24
PAGE 112

Ridge Route 50

Difficulty	3
Length	4 miles round trip
Elevation	6400/ + 600, − 600
Navigation	Road and marked trail
Time	Few hours
Season	Late December through March
USGS topo	15′ series, Pinecrest; 7.5′ series, Pinecrest
Start	Dodge Ridge Ski Area Parking loop. Follow Dodge Ridge Road to where it reaches the one-way loop of the ski area parking lot. A right turn at this point leads into the parking area at the Crabtree Trailhead.

In excellent conditions this tour can offer a thrilling descent in shin-deep snow. In poor conditions the descent requires good techniques to control your speed as you descend the ridge top.

From the trailhead ski on the spur road which weaves southwest for 0.4 mile to the intersection with Crabtree Road (**1**). Turn southeast (left) and ski up Crabtree Road for 1.1 miles. Here, you make a sharp right turn with the road (**2**). Continue on the road for 0.4 mile to a left turn (**3**).

The left turn is located at the top of the ridge on which this tour descends. Before descending you may want to ski on the road for an additional 0.1 mile to Aspen Meadow.

At the left turn leave the road and descend northwest along the ridge. Most of the descent is steep with small bumps and some trees to make the skiing even more interesting. You will intersect the Crabtree Trail Loop tour (**4**) 1.2 miles from where you started down the ridge. Ski east (right) for 0.1 mile to Crabtree Road and the spur road (**1**). Finally, follow the spur road back to the trailhead.

51 Dodge Ridge Loop

MAP 24
PAGE 112

Difficulty	4
Length	8 miles round trip
Elevation	6400/ + 1200, − 1200
Navigation	Road, map and compass
Time	Full day
Season	Late December through March
USGS topo	15′ series, Pinecrest; 7.5′ series, Pinecrest
Start	Dodge Ridge Ski Area Parking loop. Follow Dodge Ridge Road to where it reaches the one-way loop of the ski area parking lot. A right turn at this point leads into the parking area at the Crabtree Trailhead.

The most notable feature of this tour is the ski along Dodge Ridge, although you may most remember the short section through very, very dense trees. As an alternative you can make an easier tour to the ridge top via the roads, enjoy the views and solitude of the top, and then retrace your route. If you are an expert skier, you can also take a very steep route from the ridge top down into Burnt Bowl.

From the trailhead ski on the spur road which weaves southwest for 0.4 mile to the intersection with Crabtree Road (**1**). Turn southeast (left) and ski up Crabtree Road for 1.1 miles. Here, make a sharp right turn with the road (**2**) and continue for another 0.4 mile to a left turn (**3**) in the road. At the left turn the road levels and after 25 yards there will be a road junction.

At the junction you turn south (right) and ski for 0.3 mile to another junction (**5**). Here, take the fork to the southwest (right) which parallels Dodge Ridge just to its south. From the junction (**5**) it is 1.1 miles to a high point (**6**) located to the north of Peak 7175. This is a good point to turn around if you plan to retrace your route.

Along the last 1.1 miles it is easy to ski off the road to the ridge top. If you do so be careful of the steep and possibly overhung drop to the north. Burnt Bowl is an open area to the north which can be seen from the ridge. Expert skiers can descend to the bowl and intersect the Crabtree Trail Loop tour.

From the high point (**6**), descend on the road for 0.2 mile to the northwest. At this point the road turns southwest (left) and a spur continues to the northwest. Leave the road and ski along the spur. At first you will descend gradually through sparse trees, then through more dense trees and finally through an open area. At the end of the open area you will encounter a cliff (**7**). Be careful of cornices here.

At the cliff you turn west and continue along the spur for 0.4 mile until the perfect skiing terrain ends abruptly. All that you will see ahead is very, very dense trees. From this point you should ski (side step) north down the steep wooded slope for 0.3 mile in order to reach the road **(8)**. You will find a compass useful in this wooded section.

Once you have reached the road ski east (right) on it. Ahead you will encounter a four-way road intersection **(9)**. Here, the main road you intersect is Crabtree Road. Turn east (right) onto it and ski for 0.7 mile to a junction where you will pass a road on your right **(10)**. Continue on Crabtree Road for 1.1 miles to the spur road which you first skied **(1)**. Follow the spur road back to the trailhead.

Tricky terrain

52 Crabtree Road

MAP 25
PAGE 118

Difficulty	3–4
Length	Up to 16 miles round trip
Elevation	6400/Up to +2200, –2200
Navigation	Road
Time	Up to full day
Season	December through mid-April
USGS topo	15′ series, Pinecrest; 7.5′ series, Pinecrest
Start	Dodge Ridge Ski Area Parking loop. Follow Dodge Ridge Road to where it reaches the one-way loop of the ski area parking lot. A right turn at this point leads into the parking area at the Crabtree Trailhead.

A tour of any length on this road can be an enjoyable experience. Although the road leads to where Gianelli Cabin is shown on the topo, no cabin exists.

From the trailhead ski to Aspen Meadow (**1**) as described in that tour (no. 49). Past the meadow continue skiing for 0.7 mile until you reach a junction (**2**). Old Crabtree Road heads to the northeast (straight) from here. The main road, Crabtree Road, makes a sharp turn to the south (right) and is not shown on the 1956 15′ series topo.

Turn south (right) and continue skiing. Just ahead on the left side of the road will be an open area perfect for practicing telemark turns. You continue by following Crabtree Road which soon turns east (left). From this turn follow the road for 1.3 miles until you reach the road to Crabtree Camp (**3**). Continue on Crabtree Road (straight) for as far as you desire. From the road to Crabtree Camp it is 3.4 miles to where Gianelli Cabin is shown on the map.

MAP 25
PAGE 118

Old Crabtree Road 53

Difficulty	3–4
Length	Up to 14 miles round trip
Elevation	6400/Up to +2800, −2800
Navigation	Road and map
Time	Up to full day
Season	December through mid-April
USGS topo	15′ series, Pinecrest; 7.5′ series, Pinecrest (Burst Rock is 0.1 mile off map)
Start	Dodge Ridge Ski Area Parking loop. Follow Dodge Ridge Road to where it reaches the one-way loop of the ski area parking lot. A right turn at this point leads into the parking area at the Crabtree Trailhead.
End	Same as start if return is via Old Crabtree Road.

This is one of three routes to Burst Rock which is a formidable objective. The other two routes, Dodge Ridge and Gooseberry Road, are described separately. You can make a loop tour to and from Burst Rock by combining any two of the routes.

From the trailhead ski to Aspen Meadow (1) as described in that tour (no. 49). Past the meadow continue skiing for 0.7 mile until the main road, Crabtree Road, makes a turn to the south (right) (2). This new road is not shown on the 1956 15′ series topo. Do not turn; instead continue northeast (straight) on the Old Crabtree Road for 1.7 miles until you reach Peak 8147 (4). Often called "The Knob", Peak 8147 makes a fine objective. This route on Old Crabtree Road is the easiest one to "The Knob."

From Peak 8147 continue skiing east along the ridge. Although there is a road you may not be able to discern it. When you leave the peak you will descend slightly and then rise slightly to a small knob. From this knob you again descend slightly and then rise slightly to a second knob. From the second knob ski 0.1 mile east to Gooseberry Road (5) which descends north from the ridge. If Gooseberry Road is untracked you may have to look carefully for its cut. If untracked and you plan to return via Gooseberry Road, mark its location so that you will not pass by it on your return from Burst Rock.

From Gooseberry Road continue skiing east along the ridge for 2.3 miles to Burst Rock. The views to the north and south are spectacular as you ski along the ridge top.

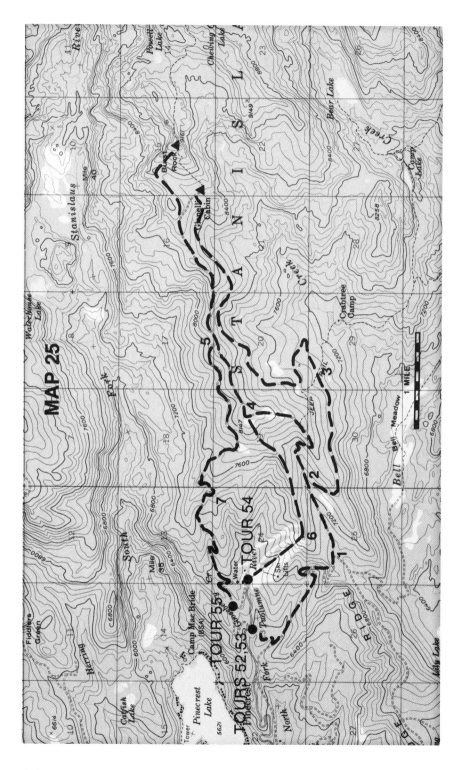

118

MAP **25**
PAGE 118

Dodge Ridge **54**

Difficulty	4
Length	Up to 10 miles round trip
Elevation	6700/Up to +2500, −2500
Navigation	Map
Time	Up to full day
Season	December through mid-April
USGS topo	15′ series, Pinecrest; 7.5′ series, Pinecrest (Burst Rock is 0.1 mile off map)
Start	Base of chairlift 5 at Dodge Ridge Ski Area. Chairlift 5 is located at the extreme east end of the ski area parking lot.
End	Same as start if return is via Dodge Ridge.

This classic tour in the Pinecrest area offers spectacular views from the ridge. It starts with a steep 800′ climb to the top of chairlift 5. The remaining 4.5 miles to Burst Rock are entirely along a ridge. On a clear day the views from the ridge are spectacular to both the north and south. It should be noted that an approved expansion of Dodge Ridge Ski Area may soon destroy this tour.

Ski to the top of chairlift 5 **(6)** making sure that you avoid the groomed slopes. From the top of the lift you ski east for 1.4 miles to Peak 8147 **(4)**. This peak is a broad high point and is sometimes referred to as "The Knob." Old Crabtree Road arrives at Peak 8147 from the south; if untracked it may be difficult to locate that roadbed because the area is quite flat. The remainder of the tour to Burst Rock is identical to the Old Crabtree Road tour (no. 53).

You can make this tour into a loop by returning to the ski area by one of two other routes. Refer to the descriptions for the Old Crabtree Road and Gooseberry Road tours.

55 Gooseberry Road

MAP 25
PAGE 118

Difficulty	3–4
Length	Up to 14 miles round trip
Elevation	6500/Up to +2700, −2700
Navigation	Road and map
Time	Up to full day
Season	December through mid-April
USGS topo	15′ series, Pinecrest; 7.5′ series, Pinecrest (Burst Rock is 0.1 mile off map)
Start	Gooseberry Trailhead located at Dodge Ridge Ski Area parking loop. Follow Dodge Ridge Road to the one-way loop of the ski area parking lot. Follow the loop to the ski area lodge and turn around as though leaving. From the lodge it is 0.3 mile to the Gooseberry Trailhead. The trailhead will be on the north (right) side of the road.
End	Same as start if return is via Gooseberry Road.

A tour on Gooseberry Road is an uphill trek which is typical of all tours heading east from the Dodge Ridge Ski Area. The redeeming factor is the return downhill run. It should be noted that an approved expansion of Dodge Ridge Ski Area may soon destroy this tour.

From the trailhead follow Gooseberry Road as it weaves to the east for 1.7 miles to Telemark Bowl (**7**). This obvious bowl is ideal for practicing downhill techniques of all skill levels.

Continue on the road for 0.3 mile until you reach a large clearing. Locate where the road exits at the south end of the clearing and follow it for 1.5 miles to a ridge (**5**).

At the ridge, Gooseberry Road joins Old Crabtree Road. Follow the Old Crabtree Road tour (no. 53) along the ridge to the east (left) to Burst Rock. From the intersection on the ridge you can return to the start by retracing your steps on Gooseberry Road or by returning via the Old Crabtree Road tour or the Dodge Ridge tour.

Following road to Burst Rock   *Kim Grandfield*

56 Herring Creek Road

MAP 26
PAGE 124

Difficulty	2–3
Length	Up to 14 miles round trip
Elevation	5900/Up to +1500, −1500
Navigation	Road
Time	Up to full day
Season	Late December through March
USGS topo	15' series, Long Barn, Pinecrest; 7.5' series, Strawberry, Pinecrest
Start	Herring Creek Road and Highway 108, 2.5 miles north of Strawberry.

A tour of any length on Herring Creek Road is relatively easy due to its gradual slope. The highlights include views into the Punch Bowl and Bull Run, and the volcanic cliffs which surround them.

From the starting point ski east on Herring Creek Road for 1.2 miles until you pass a road (1) to Leland Meadow on your left. Ski for another 1.6 miles until you pass a road (2) on your right. Continue skiing on Herring Creek Road for another 0.9 mile until you reach a ridge (3).

At the ridge several roads will intersect. Continue skiing to the northeast (right) on Herring Creek Road for 0.6 mile until you reach another road junction (4). From here you can either continue east on Herring Creek Road or turn north (left) to get a spectacular view of the Punch Bowl.

If you turn north (left), ski on this road for only 50 feet until you reach another road. Veer right onto this road which contours the hillside and after 0.2 mile you turn east (right) with the road. Continue for another 0.1 mile. At this point (there is no landmark), turn north (left) off the road and continue for 0.2 mile until you encounter the rim overlooking the Punch Bowl (5). This is a perfect spot to have lunch. Exercise caution since all the ridges above the bowls in this area can be overhung with cornices.

From the overlook above the Punch Bowl you can retrace your tracks to Herring Creek Road or continue east along the rim of the Punch Bowl. If you choose to ski along the rim, ski for 0.9 mile until you intersect Herring Creek Road again (6).

Once you are back on Herring Creek Road you can ski northeast (left) to a very very broad saddle which is the farthest point of this tour. From a point 0.1 mile before reaching the saddle you can ski west to a spectacular overlook of Bull Run.

Slab avalanche

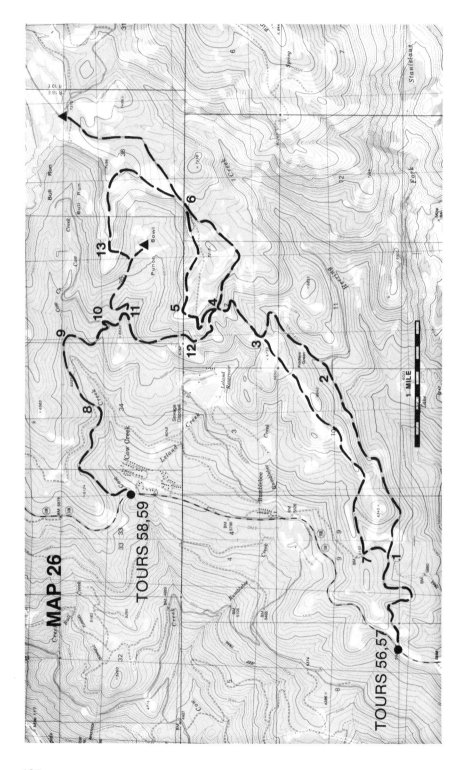

MAP 26

TOURS 58,59

TOURS 56,57

124

MAP 26
PAGE 124

Herring Creek Loop **57**

Difficulty	2
Length	7 miles round trip
Elevation	5900/+750, −750
Navigation	Road and marked trail
Time	Most of a day
Season	Late December through March
USGS topo	15′ series, Long Barn, Pinecrest; 7.5′ series, Strawberry, Pinecrest
Start	Herring Creek Road and Highway 108, 2.5 miles north of Strawberry.

By combining a section of Herring Creek Road with a parallel road, this tour forms a loop. This section of Herring Creek Road does not receive as much snowmobile use as other parts. The parallel road is normally groomed by the developers at Leland Meadow and is designated for ski touring only. For the most part this groomed portion follows an interesting route along a broad ridge top.

From the starting point ski on Herring Creek Road for 1.2 miles to a road junction (1). From this junction you can make a loop by skiing in either direction. While the clockwise direction is slightly easier, the tour described here is the counterclockwise one which offers a nice descent along the ridge top.

Continue by skiing east (straight) along Herring Creek Road for 2.5 miles to a ridge (3). Turn southwest (left) onto a groomed road.

Ski southwest on the road as it follows the ridge. You will pass to the south of Peak 6733, to the north of Peak 6642, and to the north of Peak 6345. When you are almost directly north of Peak 6345 you will pass a packed trail which descends to the north (right). Do not follow it. Instead continue west for 0.4 mile until you reach an intersection (7).

At the intersection turn south (left) onto an ungroomed road and ski for 0.2 mile until you intersect Herring Creek Road (1). You can now retrace your tracks back to the starting point.

MAP 26
PAGE 124

58 Punch Bowl

Difficulty	3
Length	7 miles round trip
Elevation	5800/ + 1050, − 1050
Navigation	Road
Time	Most of a day
Season	Late December through March
USGS topo	15' series, Pinecrest; 7.5' series, Pinecrest
Start	Junction of Cow Creek Road and Highway 108, 5.5 miles north of Strawberry and 1.0 mile before the point where the highway is closed.

For the casual skier this tour to a bowl surrounded by steep volcanic cliffs is a pleasant excursion. You will find a beautiful meadow in the center and this is a perfect place to enjoy an afternoon rest on a sunny day.

Begin this tour on the road located on the north side of Cow Creek. (Do not confuse it with the road on the south side of the creek.) Ski up this road as it gradually climbs and weaves to the east for 1.1 miles until you pass a road **(8)** on your left. Continue skiing for 0.3 mile until you pass a road on your right and then ski another 0.3 mile until you reach the bridge at Cow Creek **(9)**.

After crossing the bridge continue on the road to the south for 0.4 mile to a sharp left turn. Ski on the road 0.1 mile farther and then turn east (right) off Cow Creek Road onto a smaller road **(10)**. Continue on this road, which immediately turns south, for 0.3 mile until you reach the creek **(11)** which drains the Punch Bowl.

On the north side of the creek you will find a road to the southeast which parallels the creek. Ski on this road for about 0.1 mile and then make a sharp left turn with the road. Ski for 0.2 mile until you cross a very small ridge and follow the road as it turns southeast. Continue skiing up the road for 0.5 mile as it gradually climbs into the Punch Bowl. Once you are near the head of the bowl simply follow one of the clear paths which lead to the meadow area in the center of the bowl.

Navigating

MAP 26
PAGE 124

59 Punch Bowl Loop

Difficulty	4
Length	9 miles round trip
Elevation	5800/ + 1600, − 1600
Navigation	Road and map
Time	Full day
Season	Late December through March
USGS topo	15′ series, Pinecrest; 7.5′ series, Pinecrest
Start	Junction of Cow Creek Road and Highway 108, 5.5 miles north of Strawberry and 1.0 mile before the point where the highway is closed.

This tour climbs to the ridge top above the Punch Bowl and follows the ridge as it circles the bowl. The ridge traverse offers excellent views of the cornices which adorn the volcanic rock outcroppings and views down into the bowl.

The first part of this loop tour is identical to the Punch Bowl tour (no. 58) and you should refer to that tour description for directions to reach the creek which drains the Punch Bowl (11). Continue on the main road for 0.7 mile to a prominent point (12) which overlooks Leland Reservoir and then continue for another 0.4 mile to Herring Creek Road (4).

Just before you reach Herring Creek Road, maybe 50 feet, take the road heading northwest (left) which contours the hillside. After you have contoured for 0.2 mile you turn east (right) with the road and ski for 0.1 mile. At this point (there is no landmark) turn north (left) off the road and continue for 0.2 mile to where you will encounter the rim overlooking the Punch Bowl (5). Keep in mind that cornices are common on all the ridges in this area.

Continue by skiing east around the bowl for 0.9 mile to Herring Creek Road (6). From here, ski north following the rim of the bowl, not the road. After 0.7 mile you turn west and ski on a ridge top picking your route carefully through some trees and rock outcroppings, and avoiding the very dangerous cliffs to the north of the ridge.

The ridge you are on will eventually come to an abrupt end. From a clearing (13) located 0.2 mile before the end of the ridge descend south into the Punch Bowl. You should descend as far as possible in the open and then enter the trees. Continue descending to the south picking the best route until you intersect a very minor road. This road offers the best route out of the Punch Bowl and is the road described in the Punch Bowl tour.

Ski northwest on the road for 0.4 mile until it makes a turn to the southeast (left). If the road seems to disappear you are probably at the point where it makes the turn and you must look carefully. Make the turn and ski 0.2 mile southeast to the creek draining the Punch Bowl. Continue northwest on the road as it parallels the creek for 0.1 mile until you intersect one of the roads **(11)** you had skied earlier. Finally, retrace your route back to the starting point.

Heading down in fresh powder   *Lee Griffith*

Morning after heavy snowfall

Nordic Ski Centers

The nordic centers listed here provide ski touring services and facilities, and are a good source for current snow, weather and avalanche conditions.

KIRKWOOD CROSS-COUNTRY SKI AREA

Location	Highway 88 at Kirkwood, five miles west of Carson Pass.
Address	P.O. Box 77, Kirkwood, CA 95646
Phone	209-258-8864
Elevation	7700'

TAMARACK TOURING CENTER

Location	Highway 4 at Tamarack Lodge, two miles west of Bear Valley.
Address	P.O. Box 5041, Bear Valley, CA 95223
Phone	209-753-2080
Elevation	6900'

BEAR VALLEY NORDIC

Location	Highway 4 at Bear Valley.
Address	P.O. Box 5005, Bear Valley, CA 95223
Phone	209-753-2834
Elevation	7100'

LELAND MEADOW RESORT

Location	Highway 108 at Leland Meadow, five miles northeast of Strawberry.
Address	P.O. Box 1498, Pinecrest, CA 95346
Phone	209-965-3745
Elevation	6300'